Apostle Patty is one of the few genuine woman apostles I know. She is a daughter that I have under my spiritual covering. I am so proud of her, because she is passionate for God and His people... always ready to minister the heart of God. Her full hunger after God's heart and revelation captivates my heart. *Passionate Pursuit* is a book that outlines the hunger, and special love she feels for the Lord instilling a deeper passion for God, and His heart. As a reader, your heart will be ignited with new passion! you will come back into the first love, your life will be transformed and changed! You will have an encounter with the living God and your heart will burn with the fire of God!

Apostle Guillermo Maldonado
King Jesus International Ministries
Miami, Florida

Our spirit was so deeply stirred as we read the powerful new book, *Passionate Pursuit,* by our dear friend, Apostle Patty Valenzuela. This book is destined to help awaken the reader to a journey of freedom and deep encounters with God. It was written as a love letter to Fathers children! It teaches us that until you find yourself putting the issue of paternity to rest, you will never understand who the Father really is. It is then you will realize that God the Father has been waiting on you to crawl into His lap of love. This book will cause you to relinquish your past and dive into your *NEXT* with God. Apostle Patty shows us all that no matter who you are, you must start the journey, endure the process and put yourself in the right posture with God. What is the posture? It's at His feet, where healing and deliverance is found. We challenge you to read this book over and over. Pass it on to family, friends and co-workers. This book is destined to become a classic in the library of the revivalist! Thank you, dear friend, for allowing God to use you to write this message of hope and power!"

Pat and Karen Schatzline
Evangelists and Authors of "Rebuilding the Altar"
Remnant Ministries International

In her book, *Passionate Pursuit*, postle Patty Valenzuela takes us to the heart of the Gospel: the love of God. The Bible tells us that God is love, but so many go through life with hurt, rejection and pain, wondering whether anyone, even God Himself, loves them. People who may even work in ministry, may have an intellectual knowledge of the love of God yet have not truly experienced it. Apostle Patty takes us through her journey in a passionate pursuit of God so that we may also experience His love. Although I have served the Lord for over 25 years, this book has left me with a deep desire to get even closer to Him. For anyone who has not personally experienced the love of God, this book will touch your heart and draw you closer to Him. The love of the heavenly Father will be manifested to you. For those who have experienced the love of God, but that love has waxed cold, there will be a new passion to seek Him. I highly recommend the book *Passionate Pursuit*, as it will activate you and lead you through Scripture, testimonies, and prayer into a deeper relationship with the Father. May we all experience His deep love, and passionately pursue Him all the days of our lives.

John Laffitte, Ph.D., D.Min,
Executive VP, University of the Supernatural Ministry

Apostle Patty Valenzuela is indeed a friend, a co-disciple, and a passionate pursuer of God's presence. I am honored to write this endorsement and share with the world that she is living proof of what this book talks about. She resembles and carries so much of our spiritual father, Apostle Guillermo Maldonado's DNA. Throughout the pages of this manuscript you will encounter God in a new dimension and you will get much closer to your Creator. He is God Almighty and He is looking to reveal Himself as a person to those who desperately seek Him. You will not regret this journey, so enter it right now.

Pastor Frank Hechavarria
King Jesus International Ministries
Miami, Florida

Society tells us that role of a father is very imprtant in the life of a child, because it gives them identity, social skills and produces emotional well-being. A teenager can look for love and affirmation in all the wrong places. An adult can be attracted to the wrong company to give them the emotional love that they desperately crave.

Fatherhood is developed through responsibility in a man in three stages, manhood, husband-hood, and fatherhood. Many have jumped the process by fathering a child without the responsibility and provision of a husband first.

Pastor Patty has revealed her vulnerability in the development of her childhood traumas, that followed her into adulthood and she came from a two-parent family serving in the ministry. Thank you for your honesty and the evidence that proves, strong character is always developed from a two-parent family, but it is really established when you have a personal relationship with the Father in Heaven.

"If you, then, though you are evil, know how to give good gifts to your children, how much more will your Father in heaven give good gifts to those who ask him!" Matthew 7:11

A passionate pursuit of God will let you enquirer of Him, and as you ask, He will answer; and He will exchange your mindset for a renewed mind to do His Will.

I pray that this book seep into your spirit man and reveal the Father's will and purpose for your life.

Apostle Renny McLean
Founder of RMM, Dallas, Texas

It wasn't until I got married and had children that I realized I was a daddy's girl. My favorite phrase was "I will sweet talk my dad to do that for me." Reading Apostle Patty's book opened up all those warm feelings that I had forgotten about my relationship with my dad. However, more important than that; it made me confront my own fears and misgiving about the discipline and correction that a father will bring when he loves you. There is a deficit of knowledge and experience for this generation who don't know the relationship of a father, and our Heavenly Father. I've had the pleasure of standing beside Apostle Patty in worship, and we are both passionate in our expression of love in the presence of God. There is a natural abandonment of self, and an awareness of where we are in the heavens not on earth; in the height of worship. I pray that this book will take you on a journey of discovery and passionate pursuit of our eternal father's love and affirmation of who you are becoming in Him. There is no longer a hidden mystery about worship, there is a constant unveiling in His Presence of who He has called you to become.

Thank you in advance Pastor Patricia for awakening a hunger for the presence of God.

Prophet Marina McLean
Co-Founder of RMM, Dallas Texas

It is our joy to recommend to you Apostle Patty Valenzuela's book *Passionate Pursuit*. The message and heart of this book becomes contagious as you are caught up in her genuine desire to inspire you to join her as she unreservedly seeks the presence of her Heavenly Father. This is not just another "how to" book but rather an invitation to take an unfiltered journey with Apostle Valenzuela as God has lovingly taken her from brokenness to wholeness and the intimacy of his presence. *Passionate Pursuit,* will challenge and encourage any Christian at any level to renew their desire to passionately seek and encounter the presence of their loving Heavenly Father. It is from the heart that Apostle has written this message for all who will, to join her in a pursuit and love for our Father.

Pastors George and Phyllis Sawyer
Calvary Assembly
Decatur, Alabama

I know Apostle Patty Valenzuela to be a mighty woman of God. She is also a dear friend. This allows me a unique perspective into her life and the genuine impact of her ministry at El Paso, Texas as well as around the world. Apostle Patty is passionate for the presence of God and is an apostolic voice that heralds and demonstrates not only supernatural power of God in prophecy, healing, and miracles but also manifests His relentless, eternal love as the Heavenly Father.

Apostle Patty's new book, *Passionate Pursuit*, is full of truth and revelation concerning the loving, perfect fatherhood of God that will transform the way the readers see God and themselves as they fully embrace their identity as His sons and daughters. This new book is particularly powerful because Apostle Patty not only teaches the truth of the Word – she continually experiences it. With testimonies from her own life, *Passionate Pursuit* leads readers to an encounter with the fatherhood of God and His supernatural love that will be life-changing and radically impact their personal, family, and even ministerial lives. As an apostle, pastor, author, wife, and mother, Apostle Patty has learned how to overcome countless obstacles and set-backs and how to trust and submit to God through the challenges and processes of life to emerge as a powerful, anointed voice to this generation. I wholeheartedly recommend this book to men and women of all ages, leaders and casual church goers alike, as I know God will use *Passionate Pursuit* to open the eyes of their understanding, deliver them of rejection and of being bound to pleasing others, and will ignite them with a passion for their Heavenly Father that will never die!

Minister and Teacher Letty Laffitte,
University of the Supernatural Ministry
King Jesus International Ministry
Miami, FL

Growing up in ministry and actually having ministered in thousands of churches around the world, I've come to the place where I really want to see the "authentic moves of God." God will trust this move in the hands and hearts of mature and anointed people. Apostle Patty Valenzuela is what I believe is an example woman of God. She has a spirit like Deborah in the Bible who was a warrior and a prophet, while also having the anointing and influence like Queen Esther. She has a great marriage, two powerful daughters, and the love and respect of a powerful church which has now morphed into a powerful ministry that is reaching around the world. This book, *Passionate Pursuit,* is truly from the heart of God. The transparency and vulnerability Apostle Patty shows disarms you as you become enthralled with her story. The revelation she shares is both divine and practical. This book brings the "Nowness of God" into the reality of our lives. This book for people who have just met the Lord or people who have walked with the Lord for many years. We can never pursue God with a "business as usual" attitude. I wholeheartedly recommend this book to my friends and those who truly hunger for God. Great job Apostle Patty.

Apostle Dwayne Swilley
Duane Swilley Ministries

This book is a gift from God to draw you into a deeper, more fulfilling relationship with your Heavenly Father. The author's passion for God's presence is infectious and you will find yourself thirsting for a fresh touch of His Spirit. Apostle Patty writes with heart-felt honesty about deep longings she felt that were never satisfied until she was engulfed in the love of God. She will show you how you too can experience that same heavenly love in ways you never thought possible. This book is for anyone who wants to be refreshed, renewed, re-fired. It will take you on a journey to greater intimacy with the Lord and to true fulfillment.

Jo Naughton, Founder, Healed for Life
Pastor, Harvest Church London, UK

Passionate Pursuit by Patricia Valenzuela is a battle cry for you to step out of the ordinary and live differently. It's a blueprint for a life full of pursuit of God's presence.

Shaneen Clarke
International speaker, Author,
Parton of Hope Gardens Charity

Pastor Patty Valenzuela really knows and loves Jesus with all of her heart. She wants the whole body of Christ to experience the intimacy that she experiences daily. Get ready to have your spiritual appetite whet for more of Him. As you read, she will take you on a journey to have your fire and passion rekindled. Get ready to go deeper. We all need it. Thank you, Apostle Patty, for writing this book. -

Pastor Deborah Berteau
The House Modesto

*Passionately pursuing the God that is
in passionate pursuit of you*

PASSIONATE
PURSUIT

Patty Valenzuela

ISBN: 978-1-54391-312-5 (print)
ISBN: 978-1-54391-313-2 (ebook)

This book is dedicated to my Heavenly Father.

You're my Hero, my Strength, and the One
in whom I've always taken refuge;
You have taught me everything...I will
always passionately pursue You!

ACKNOWLEDGMENTS

My husband, Andy, who has supported me in ministry, encouraged me and has taught me how to rise in the midst of affliction. You have taught me how to be a strong warrior, I thank you for running this race with me; I love you.

My precious daughters Andrea and Jaklyn, who have sacrificed so much for the advancement of the Kingdom of God. Thank you for being the best daughters I could have asked for, I love you girls so much.

Pastor Norma Carnera, thank you for making this book possible; thank you for being my Johnathan. I respect and love you greatly.

Pastor Erica Soto, thank you for your careful attention to detail. Thank you for your faithful work and for being my Nehemiah. I love you dearly.

Pastor Jackie Arteaga, thank you for being so gifted in all you do. You are such an asset, not only to me and Ignite Movement, but to the Kingdom of God. I love you so much.

Ignite Movement Church, thank you for being the best family a pastor could ask for! Thank you for loving me and for praying for me the way you do!

My dad, Pastor Noel Jimenez, thank you for pioneering and teaching me the greatest lessons in life. For instilling in me that quitting is not an option.

My mom, Pastor Irene Jimenez, thank you for your love affection and teaching me that everything is possible with God.

My sisters, Laura and Millie, thank you for taking care of me in my upbringing and teaching me that at the end of all trials - family remains.

Grama Lucy, you are in such a better place now. I am so grateful to God for the wonderful cheerleader He gave me in you! Thank you for always encouraging me. You will be missed.

To all my Kingdom friends, thank you for being a part of my life. Each one of you has highlighted different aspects of the Kingdom in such a powerful way, and in doing so, it has brought much enrichment and blessing to my life. I love you all dearly.

My spiritual father, Apostle Guillermo Maldonado, thank you for your instruction and love.

Thank you for stretching me and pushing me to be the best me I could be.

CONTENTS

THE PURSUIT INTRODUCED...

I WASHED THE produce in my sink mechanically. My thoughts drifted from the task at hand—making dinner for my family—to the recent intimate meeting I had. It's like I couldn't get enough, I missed him, missed the closeness, his voice, and the things he told me... Every time I would seek him out and I closed my eyes I would just utterly and completely lose myself in him. There really was no other experience like it...I missed him. I wanted to be near him again.

I could hear the water running in the sink. But my thoughts were on him...

Tears welled up in the corner of my eyes. I just wanted to run back into his arms. Nothing on earth made me feel the way I felt when I was with him. So safe, so loved, so cherished...

There was an ache inside of me. I wanted to be near him. I needed be near him.

I was lovesick.

I felt him draw near. It was as if my thoughts, my longing for more of him summoned him. I felt him lovingly wrap himself around me.

This may sound like the beginning of a romance novel. To some extent it is. It is a beautiful romance, a love story. It's a love that I found after many years of fear, insecurity, rejection, letdowns and pain.

This love makes any grown woman, or man for that matter, feel like a child in their daddy's arms. It's perfect, complete, you don't have to speak because He knows exactly what you are feeling—your

1

tears become words while His soft touch heals your every wound, every pain.

God's love and what has manifested in my life because of His love is the reason for my passionate pursuit of Him early every morning and at any given moment of the day. Yes, it is true, one encounter with God can be life transforming, but if *one* encounter can do that—what would our lives look like if we relentlessly and passionately pursue this loving, life transforming God?

We are very much a part of a fatherless generation. Many people grow up without a father and they are void of a father's love, a father's protection, his approval or affirmation. When this happens, we go throughout our lives looking for approval, for love for affirmation from just about anyone that will give it to us.

There are so many boys and girls locked up within adult bodies seeking that love, that affirmation of a father. Sadly, oftentimes because there was no one around to cheer us on we lack the motivation to achieve anything. So, we end up living a life that is so short of what God had dreamed for us. Directly on the opposite pole of this, yet just as damaging is a life that strives to gain the approval of man. So, we overachieve, yet with trophies in hand, we still feel empty and sad. The desire to be loved, profoundly and exclusively loved is something we all innately carry within us.

It was something I so craved as a child that was plagued with fear. I dreaded nighttime during my grade school years. Darkness caused me to tremble uncontrollably in my bed and sleep walk sometimes even into my neighbor's yards in the middle of the night.

This love was something I would ache for as a teen as I looked out to the stands during the intensity of a soccer game searching for someone to cheer me on…only to discover no one that mattered was at my game. It was something I finally discovered as an adult in the middle of one of the biggest trials of my life, it wasn't at a church where I experienced this, it was in my bedroom; I cried out to God in my pain, despair and abandonment. I had experienced God's love before, I believe there are many layers, if you will, to His love. But what I experienced that day transformed my life forever. God's love and affirmation overwhelmed me that afternoon in my room and I was not the same.

God's love…nothing in my life has compared to it. His love rescued me and now I'm just simply addicted to it.

Everyone needs this love. Many of us can become hard-hearted by life's situations: abandonment, abuse, divorce, death of loved ones, sickness—the list does go on. It doesn't matter how hardened we are, or how cold we have become or how accustomed we are to living without affection or without fellowship; we all need this love.

There are many things, that today as an adult I understand, things that perhaps in my childhood I did not. I understand that my parents did the best they could with what they had and knew. They both dealt with their own burdens and they were both very much in need of a savior. And my sisters, well, they coped with things in our family in their own way. As a child, I recall observing some of my friends' families, having a faint longing for what it appeared that they had—yes, even as a child my enemy made the grass look greener on the other side…

Despite the fact that I grew up in a home with both parents and two sisters, I felt very lonely. On the outside, it appeared I had everything— good grades, ran for homecoming queen and won, tried out for my school's beauty pageant and won "Most Beautiful", played soccer with everything I had, was drum major for the high school marching band…I was seeking affirmation so badly. On the inside though, I was empty, so empty and so lonely and afraid. The emptiness I sought to fill with boyfriends seemed to get bigger and deeper after each relationship ended…

Years later, I find myself doing ministry alongside my dad, and on the outside, it all looked good. My dad was pastoring a church that was seemingly thriving and I was very much a part of it. I'm just being real here, you know just because one is in ministry does not mean that everything's perfect. (As a matter of fact, even before I was called to serve in ministry I had seen things at some of the first churches I attended that left me quite disappointed.) Ministry does not perfect things--yes, my dad served God, yes, he was the senior pastor of a growing church, and *yes, the hunger I had as a little girl to be affirmed and held and protected was still there*...except now, I myself, was in ministry leading a growing youth group—composed of many kids that also needed the affirmation of a father.

I have always been a seeker, a hunter. If I don't find a solution in one place, I don't conform—I keep hunting. If I am told no, that it cannot be done, that it's never been done—I keep pushing, I keep knocking. That's just me. So naturally, as a youth pastor, I wanted more for my youth group; I wanted to reach a generation for God, a generation that would be sold out and on fire for God. I went to established youth ministries for help, piling our entire youth group in vans, driving them to Phoenix, Los Angeles, Dallas and San Antonio, all with the purpose to learn and grow. But in my search, I discovered I still had that nasty old feeling I had as a child. That longing, that emptiness, no matter how much ministry I did, it was still there.

Rejection is one of the enemy's weapons of choice to hold people hostage. It seemed my life had everything lined up for the perfect recipe for me to be a casualty of rejection. I was a young inexperienced female pastor leading a group of teens. In my service and all the serving that I did—even as a young teen in high, school I didn't realize that as I longed to please others, my peers, my teachers, my dad—the one I really wanted to please was my Heavenly Father. That had been written in me since before the foundation of time.

It seemed the enemy had strategized the perfect recipe for my destruction. In the middle of my seeking affirmation for myself and for the young group I was leading, and after 17 years of faithful service—that was under constant opposition—I found myself completely separated and abandoned by my family and by the church where I had toiled the ground and sown many seeds. Although, at the time it felt like a sudden move, something unexpected, it was actually something that had been deteriorating for quite some time.

These were times of deep sadness for me, and loss—I was completely at a loss for words, for explanation, for anything really because of the uncertain future I was now facing.

I had had other encounters with God, I had heard God's voice, I had felt His presence, but it wasn't until I had this particular encounter as I cried out to God in my abandonment and despair that I had felt God's supernatural love pour over me. I felt Him enter my bedroom; I perceived His steps on my rug approaching me. I was completely enraptured my Father's love that gently removed the pain and the fear I had carried for years but had also intensified during the time of my ministering with my dad. Since that encounter I have never lost my fire for God. Did all my problems magically go away after this encounter? No—but one thing I can assure you is that in the season where doubt could have engulfed me, I didn't allow my fire for God to be put out—it in fact burned stronger, more fervently for Him.

In all my seeking for the affirmation of my earthly father, what I came into and discovered was that the affirmation of my Heavenly Father caused such a revolution in my life that I consider it my mandate to restore the people back to the Father. There are two things I know and have experienced that can transform and change the direction of an individual's life forever—the first being salvation, and the second is having the revelation that God *is your Father*. There is no greater reward for me than when people experience the Father's love and have an encounter with Him.

Beloved reader, let me take you by the hand; come, let me let you experience this amazing journey into the Father's heart as you read the pages of this book; let me introduce you to this wonderful Person, let me take you into our Daddy's presence, into the place where I have been, where He has affirmed, changed and healed my heart from every wound.

Countless times in my life I could have quit because of the pain, the disappointments, the opposition and the oppression that threatened to take my very breath away—but I didn't.

Why? Why could I not bring myself to give up and quit? For the simple reason that I had been with my Father, that I had heard His voice, that I had been face to face with Him. How could one quit on a Father that tells you He loves you? I couldn't. I wouldn't. I won't.

In this book, I want to take you on a journey; a journey that will awaken a deep desire in you to always be in a passionate pursuit of this loving Father. In this book, you will see the evidence of the Father's love threaded about in each page —because His love has been poured out in every area of my life and He wants to pour it over you! I want to help you rekindle your hunger for God and usher you into dimensions of His love where all fear is broken off. You will learn how to be utterly dependent on God in every circumstance— to where your only desire is to please the King—even in the midst of a difficult process. You will learn how to persevere and get that second wind that will not allow you to quit so that you reach your God-designed purpose and destiny. I want to lead you to a place in the Father's presence where every rejection you have ever dealt with will fall off of you and the broken places of your life are restored. I want to lead you to have a zeal and fire for God no matter what season or process you are going through. No matter what you see, who offended you, or what pain you're carrying you don't have to lose your fire for God.

This book is written for every little girl that wanted to dance a waltz on her daddy's feet. It is written for the little boy that waited for his papa to come home from work in the evening hours when the shadows grow longer and scarier… for the little girl that cried out to be rescued in the darkest of nights, to be held and quieted in strong loving arms… This book is for every son whose heart craved playing ball with their dad, for every young man that hungered for the approving nod of a father, for every son, for every daughter that yearns to hear the Father say, "I approve of you, My child."

HUNGER FOR GOD

You are what you eat...

"As the deer pants for streams of water,
so my soul pants for you, my God.
My soul thirsts for God, for the living God.
When can I go and meet with God?"

Psalm 42:1-2 (NIV)

THERE WAS A soft glow to the ornately decorated dining hall. A long table was lavishly set with every kind of delicacy imaginable. Finely cut fruit from exotic parts of the world towered over rich meats and cheeses; pastries looked more like art work than something edible. The aroma heightened my awareness of the hunger pangs I had. I was so desperately hungry, a fallen crumb underneath the table I would have gladly taken. My eyes traveled the length of the table to the end. There He sat, at the head of the table, smiling warmly, lovingly. His hand extended as He summoned me to dine with Him...

...God has prepared a banquet for us and a feast of His presence. Yes, a feast of His presence: joy, peace, love, rest, refreshing...

anything we can imagine in our human minds fall short of the spiritual feast we are invited to dine at.

As rich and tasty as this feast may be, however, if we are full it won't be appetizing to us. Perhaps it has happened to you. You snack on different things before dinner time and when you sit to eat—you're really not that hungry. As good as the food may look, you take a few bites, yet you don't really enjoy your dinner because your hunger has been satisfied with something else.

The normal or shall I say healthy state of a Christian should be a continual hunger for God. Spiritual hunger comes naturally when we first give our lives to Jesus. When we first come to Jesus, everything is new and we love this newness. It's like when we begin a romantic relationship. We just want to spend time with the person, we want to be near them, we love to hear their voice, we smile when we read their love letters…and when we are face to face there is little else we would rather be doing.

That's exactly how it is with Jesus. When we first invite Jesus into our lives we just want to spend time at church, because we want everything that is associated with Him and anything that brings us closer to Him. We love to hear the preached Word, because we feel Him speaking to us directly—in a church full of people we are certain the word is just for us. When we read the Word, we rejoice at His great love for us. We feel as if we cannot get enough of God of His word, of His presence…

This is how spiritual hunger is manifested.

It is manifested by reading the Word of God, pursuing His presence, by seeking time alone with Him, to meditate, pray and worship. When we first come to Jesus, a strong craving and desire for Him is awakened. And just like physical hunger, when we don't feed ourselves with Him, there is a discomfort—a weakness caused by this lack of spiritual food with the strong desire to eat. There are times sadly, when the newness and excitement of a relationship ends. The ugly spirit of familiarity corrodes the wonder and awe once felt and the hunger that was once so strong, is no longer present in our lives.

There are two main reasons for the lack of hunger for God, the first being "snacking." Do you know someone that's a snacker? They are constantly munching on something, chips, popcorn, candy, sweets…and when the time comes to sit down for a solid healthy meal they really don't eat—because they aren't hungry—the snacks have satisfied them.

If we aren't careful, distractions will creep into our lives and remove our hunger for God; these distractions can be social media, our cell phones and entertainment. It's so easy to spend an hour on Facebook or text messaging! We can also end up feeding on other things—we feed on fear, on anxiety. Perhaps in the past when you first came to Jesus and problems arose, your first response was to read your Word, to pray and declare His promises over your situation. When problems arise now, however, when that unexpected hospital bill comes, you reach into your pantry and pull out reasoning, fear and stress, instead of feeding on God and meditating how in the past He has come through for you.

Perhaps your snacking is not stress or worry, perhaps yours is shopping or people. As a matter of fact, there is a woman reading this book, you feel lonely, you are going through a divorce and you used to run to God, but now instead you are trying to fill the void with shopping. Dear woman, there is no amount of clothing, purses or shoes that can satisfy the way that God can. Only God can fill the void and heal your pain. He wants to meet with you, hold you close and heal your wounds. The emptiness in our soul that life situations bring, that trials or problems bring can only be filled by God.

We were each created with an innate desire to have fellowship with God. To walk with Him, talk with Him—to live our daily lives with him, when we don't desire this we are either in sin or have allowed other things to take the place of God; the result being is that our appetite for Him is dull and we no longer passion for Him.

God can lay out the best banquet, with the richest foods and delicacies—but if we are not hungry—if God's banquet isn't appetizing to us anymore, we are either snacking on something else or sick.

Spiritual sickness is another reason why we lack hunger for God. Have you ever been so sick physically that you have no appetite for food? You cannot even taste or smell your food because your nose is congested. Or worse still, the sight or smell of food causes nausea and therefore you refuse to eat. One of the signs that we have lost passion and fire for God is that we are no longer hungry for the things of God. We don't pursue Him anymore, we don't crave Him anymore and we don't desire Him anymore…

There are several reasons for the loss of spiritual appetite. One of the reasons is unbelief.

Unbelief is one of the greatest spiritual sicknesses that we can have. The attitude of, "Ah, what for? I've tried getting close to God but nothing happens. I don't feel anything and He certainly hasn't answered me, so why even try?" When we pursue God, we must *believe* that He will respond to us. Hebrews 11:6 says, "And it is impossible to please God without faith. Anyone who wants to come to him must believe that God exists and that he rewards those who sincerely seek him." (NIV)

Another reason for the loss of spiritual appetite is sin. Sin separates us from presence of God. Sin causes us to have strange fire before God. God loves fire. God is fire. The Bible says He is a consuming fire. We are set ablaze when we passionately love God with all that we are. He doesn't accept just any fire though, dear reader. The Bible calls us to have a pure fire for God, not a strange fire. Strange fire like the one that the sons of Aaron offered in the book of Leviticus 10: 1-2 does not fool God. These men, Aaron's sons, were disobedient to the Lord's instructions, and they ended up offering a strange sacrifice before the Lord; verse 2 says, "So fire came out from the presence of the Lord and consumed them, and they died before the Lord." (NIV) We can go to church, sing our songs, dance our dance, and shout "Amen!" But if there is something off in our lives, if there is hidden sin in our lives, all that fire will do nothing for us. In fact, it will eventually destroy us just like it did to Aaron's sons.

To stay hungry for God we must recognize that we have been snacking, eating junk food or even have been spiritually sick. To stay hungry, we must *realize that only God can satisfy us—nothing else satisfies.* Other things, people, possessions, achievements may fill us for a time but will not have the lasting satisfaction that only God can give us. When we live in this realization, we love God with all our heart, our soul and our mind as Jesus commands us to do in Matthew 22:37, "Jesus replied: Love the Lord your God with all your heart and with all your soul and with all your mind." (NIV)

Beloved, God wants us to enjoy the full eating experience! When we eat we don't just merely swallow food for the sake of nourishment—although we are nourished to the full when we eat at His table. Our Heavenly Father wants us to savor Him, to taste and experience the different qualities, blessings and attributes found in Him. That's why the Word of God tells us to *taste* and see that the Lord is good, (Psalm 34:8). To taste something in the natural we must put it in our mouth and experience the flavor and the texture; if it is something we really enjoy we savor it in our mouths so that our taste buds can prolong the experience of the flavor.

Tasting in the spirit is very similar to experiencing the nature of God. Tasting God, His goodness, His love, His presence, His glory—really does leave you craving for more. When we "taste" God it really is none other than having an encounter with Him; and because there really is no other feeling on earth when you encounter God this becomes a catalyst for a more passionate pursuit of Him. Think about it dear reader, is there anything that can possibly compare to having an intimate experience, an intimate meeting with Almighty God?

I have tasted God through prayer, when I have had a need and instead of reaching for something or someone else, I go to Him in prayer, I experience how good, how tasty He is because in the middle of my need there is peace, and an assurance that He has heard me. I've tasted Him in worship, when I am utterly and completely lost in His presence in worship and what I am feeding on is not anything that is of this world but I feel as if I am in His chambers, enjoying the richest of my King's feast with Him. I taste God by hearing, reading and studying His word and chewing on it, savoring the taste and getting it in my spirit. Very much as a chef does when trying to discover what ingredients are used in a dish that is presented to him. I taste God when I am aware of His presence while I'm at the gym or at the store.

When I pursue God, I sit down to eat at His table. I take the time to enjoy my meal with Him. I'm not talking drive-thru here. God is not a drive-thru kind of God. He is not a microwave meal kind of God either—and He doesn't want us to rush through our meal either; He doesn't want us standing by the kitchen counter while we eat as we multi-task other things. No, His desire is that we *dine with Him*. That we sit and converse while we enjoy what He has prepared for us —I am speaking to a young mom, you are reading this page and as you read you are feeling the presence of God so strong, He is inviting you to dine with Him at this moment. Put the book down, your children are at school, the chores can wait…go dine with Him.

As we recognize our need for Him, it is that very yearning within us that motivates us to pursue Him. When we pursue Him, we find Him. God doesn't hide from us—Jeremiah 29:13 assures us that when we seek Him, we will find Him when we seek Him with all our heart. "And ye shall seek me, and find me, when ye shall search for me with all your heart." (KJV) This beautiful romance, this honeymoon with God never has to end. Because with God, there is always more and it increasingly gets better. As we get to know Him, we experience and see His goodness, love, beauty, perfection and holiness.

The psalmist expresses something in chapter 73: 25-26, he says:

"Whom have I in heaven but you?

And earth has nothing I desire besides you.
My flesh and my heart may fail, but God is the strength
of my heart and my portion forever." (NIV)

Are you one among those that desire nothing on earth besides God? Are you satisfied with a mere taste of Him? Is it enough for you to have a visitation or just a touch from God? Are we truly passionate and hungry for God?

Let's define hunger so that we know what hunger is:
Hunger— a strong desire or craving; a yearning; a longing; a thirst; to be restless; a painful longing; wishing with one's whole heart and striving to attain it; an unsatisfied appetite; steadfastness.

Now, let's take a look at what passion is:
Passion—a strong and barely controllable emotion; intense drive; appetite; strong craving; strong desire; strong longing; yearning; zeal; enthusiasm.

This should give us an indication if we are passionately pursuing God or if we have become monotonous or mechanically going through the motions in our relationship with Him.

We cannot survive with one meal our whole lives! That would be impossible! We would die of starvation and dehydration. Just as a physical body needs food to survive, so our spirit needs God to thrive. It is critical that we develop and maintain a lifestyle of hunger and passionately pursuing God daily.

Is all this talk of "food" making you hungry beloved? That is my prayer. There is something interesting that has happened in my home on more than one occasion. I will be preparing dinner while my husband is busy doing something else. He will pass by the kitchen when I first start to pull my ingredients out of the fridge. "Are you hungry?" I'll ask him. He walks by, determined to finish the task at hand. "No, not really but thanks," he responds. I know though, that the moment the smell of our dinner reaches his nostrils he will quickly change his mind.

In the natural a craving for food can be stirred up by smelling it, by remembering how something tasted, or even by watching the ever-popular cooking programs.

Perhaps you may be a bit frustrated because you really want to experience God; you want the hunger for God that I have been describing. There is hope! We don't have to be satisfied and conformed to a stagnant relationship with God. There is hope; there is an answer to returning to our first love. We can return to having excitement within us to seek God! We can go back and stir our love for God up!

Even as you're reading this you may be missing that touch of God that you once had. The warmth you felt all over your body as He drew near to you, the sweet peace of His presence or His love that melted your heart...

To return to this hunger the first thing we must begin to do is:

- Miss Him.

When we miss something, it's caused by the realization of the absence of something. This realization reminds us how the presence was once in our lives and is no longer there.

Beloved reader, you need to start missing the presence of God. Perhaps you are being reminded of the very presence of God that you once enjoyed...when He used to touch you, what you felt at the altar when you first accepted Jesus. You are remembering when God's presence came and saturated your room when you used to seek Him.

If we want passion back, we need to start missing him. Do you remember how you felt so secure as you closed your eyes and spoke to Him? How at times you were so lost in His presence you just knew He was right in front of you even if you couldn't see Him. Do you remember the warm waves of His presence coming over you and how at that moment nothing mattered? All your pain, your sadness, your worries disappeared...Do you remember how it didn't matter if others saw the tears on your face as you worshiped Him at the altar because at that moment in time it was just you and Him and nothing else existed.

We must go back to missing God. We must be *aware* of God's presence, with this we will avoid what happened to Jacob. In Genesis 28:16, God visited Jacob in a dream, he saw angels ascending and descending! Yet when he awoke he said, "...Surely the Lord is in this place; and I knew it not." (KJV) What a terrible thing, for us to be in the very presence of God and not know it.

David on the other hand was a man whose life was one of continual pursuit of God. He loved God so passionately that he was always aware of God's nearness to him. "I am always aware of the Lord's presence; he is near, and nothing can shake me." (Psalm 16:8 GNT). Perhaps sin drove you away from His presence; you mustn't let that keep you from Him! David sinned, he missed the mark terribly, but he couldn't bear the gaping emptiness he felt within Him because He didn't have the presence of God with him anymore. David was desperate, and he cried out to God in desperation for Him, "Cast me not away from thy presence; and take not thy holy spirit from me." (Psalm 51:11 KJV). We must cry out and start missing God like David did. There was something inside of David, he missed God and was aware of that. We must have a heart like David, that even if he missed the mark, even if he sinned he was aware of his desperate need for God. Perhaps it is sin that has separated you from God's presence; you need to cry out like David. Go ahead, cry out to Him and tell Him, "I MISS YOU GOD!"

Another thing we can do to regain a hunger for God is:

• Pray for it.

Did you know that the simple desire to seek God is a gift from God? Jesus said in John 6:44, that no one can come to him unless the Father who sent him draws them to God. When we pray for spiritual hunger it really is the Father that is drawing us to Him, we are praying God's will when we pray for a hunger for God. Don't stop praying for it until you see your breakthrough. God wants to be pursued by you, ask for His presence, seek for His presence and knock every door down till you get to His presence! (Luke 11:9) You may also want to consider fasting, a time to separate yourself to seek God. Fasting is something that allows us to become very sensitive to the presence of God.

The next thing you can do is:

- Remember it.

In the book of Revelation 2:4-5, Jesus told the Ephesian church "you have forsaken your first love...remember the height from which you have fallen." (NIV)

A hunger and desire for God can be stirred up by remembering a time when you were pursuing God. Perhaps it is when you first came to God, when you first invited Him into your life. I'm certain that as you read this, images are coming to you, reminding you of a time when you used to go off by yourself to seek that alone time with God. Perhaps you would wake up before everyone else in your home to read your Bible and meditate on God's word before your day started.

Now it's time to:

- Catch it!

Passion is contagious, spiritual hunger is contagious. I love to get around my pastors, Apostle Guillermo and Prophet Ana Maldonado. They are so passionate about pursuing God, about seeking God's presence. Every time I get near them I feel closer to God myself and can't wait to go and seek an encounter with Him! When we surround ourselves with people who pursue and love God, we are sure to catch a hunger for God in our lives.

Jackie Arteaga, a pastor and lead evangelist at Ignite Movement Church shares her testimony on how she caught the hunger and passion for God in her life:

I grew up in the church, my dad used to be a preacher; my mother's grandfather had been one of the founders of the church I attended. Church was very much a part of my life; it was part of my culture. Sadly, I found myself going through the motions, believing Jesus was a historical figure, I was full of religion, and I had little faith. My entire life I had gone to church, I knew the Bible stories, but Christianity seemed so fictional. My life seemed no different than other teenagers who were raised outside the church. At the age of 16, I was bound to anger, hate, unforgiveness, and felt my life had no purpose. I remember crying out to God, closing my eyes and saying, "God, if you're real, change my life. Do something only you can do, set me free!" That same week, as I was sitting outside school waiting for my ride, a young man approached me and invited me to Ignite Movement Church. I was not interested in attending because I was tired of church, I wanted something genuine, and I was looking for something real, not another religion. Within the following days, I felt such a tug upon my life, that I decided to visit the church I had been invited to, little did I know my life was about to be transformed.

Walking into the church I saw so many young people praising and worshipping God. I thought to myself, "How could this be? How can someone love a God they can't see? Is this even real?" When the preaching started I saw Apostle Patty Valenzuela for the first time, as she began to preach, everything she was saying applied to my life. I could not comprehend how it seemed as if she was preaching specifically to me, I knew that wasn't the case because I did not know anyone at that church. As she was speaking on the power of the Blood of Jesus, I began to feel the presence of God! I could not understand what I was experiencing, I felt overwhelmed by the love of God, to the point where nothing else mattered but I just wanted to know the Father. At that point, I realized I had never known God, I had just known about Him. That night I ran out of church, my life had been marked by the presence of God! The following week I was desperate to go back to church, I wanted to encounter God again! I felt something burning inside of me; I knew I had found my answer! I had found what was missing in my life, it's like if a void in my heart was filled! The second time I was at church, I began to weep and I felt walls in my life break down, it was as if my heart had softened, I was not afraid to hold back my tears and surrender to God. As I drove home that night, I came to a red light and felt heat all over my body and such a love of God; I repented and reconciled my life to God.

The days that followed marked my life. I had such desperation to know God, to read the Bible, to pray, and to tell others about Jesus. I had found God and no one had to tell me God was real but I had experienced Him for myself. God had become my reality and the hunger I felt for Him continued to grow. Seeing the passion upon Pastor Andy and Apostle Patty for God, I decided to make Ignite Movement my church. Time did not quench my hunger for God but only allowed me to know God more. I could not be still or keep the gospel to myself but everywhere I went I would testify and preach the gospel. I had such a passion to win the lost, to remove the veils of religion, to show the world that Jesus was not dead! I remember being in high school and preaching the gospel in my classrooms, to my teachers, praying for my classmates at school, even being in line about to graduate and sharing the gospel with those around me.

I have been activated to operate in the supernatural power of God by my pastors. Because of this, I am able to reach more people. I remember going to our local hospital emergency room with some friends from church and praying for the sick. People started clearing out of the ER because they were getting healed! With religion out of the way, I have been able to recognize the need others have for Jesus. God has used me in miracles, healings, in the prophetic, and word of knowledge. The passion for God that burns inside of me allows me to be unafraid when preaching the gospel, to be bold and daring, to care more for the salvation of others than for my reputation. My life has never been the same, I'm now 23 and it's been almost 7 years that I've been living for God and the passion I have for Him only continues to grow. I now lead the evangelism and media ministry at Ignite Movement and I've had the honor of seeing hundreds of souls come to God. I recently led an outreach in our city and witnessed up to 4,500 souls get saved within hours! I know none of this would have been possible without a continuous burning passion for God.

Passion and hunger for God causes us to operate in the supernatural, in miracles, in signs and in wonders. Daniel 11:32 says, "...but the people that do know their God, shall be strong, and do exploits." (KJV)

My passion for God, my hunger and my fire for God has led us to see countless healings and miracles. I remember on one occasion in one of our *Supernatural Nights* services, I released a word of knowledge. The Lord had shown me that there was a man and a woman present; they were desperate because they had a child that was very sick in the hospital. Moments later a couple came up for prayer. Their newborn baby was indeed very sick; he had been born with his umbilical cord wrapped around his neck, which caused health complications. The parents had initially been given a bleak diagnosis—that their baby would not be able to leave the hospital without two tubes connected to his little body, one for his throat to help him breathe and another tube through which he would be fed.

Putting a demand in heaven, with the expectation to see the supernatural healing power of God manifest in this baby, we laid hands on a cloth, anointed it, and prayed for the baby, instructing the parents to place the cloth on their baby as soon as they returned to the hospital where their baby was at. Immediately after the couple placed the cloth on the baby, the swelling in his body disappeared; this enabled him to begin eating on his own! A short two weeks after, the pediatrician told the parents that their baby was developing at a normal pace! Had God's supernatural power not intervened, this baby would be on life support today, but because of God's healing power, today the child is eating and breathing on his own, and no tubes or machines are connected to him!

Another way to return to hunger for God is to begin to worship Him. One definition of worship is to *lean forward and to kiss the face of God.*

- Worship

A new worship song can stir up a desire to spend time with Him. It's like listening to the perfect love song, and the words are driving you to have an intimate meeting with your Beloved. Go ahead, play that worship song, begin this romantic relationship with God again—start that communication with Him again.

Stop talking about it, stop hoping and wishing, now:

- Act on it!

We really need to taste and savor God. The more we encounter His presence the more we will hunger for Him.

I'm going to give you an opportunity to implement the last point. *Act on it*—go ahead go and find a place where you can be left alone, turn up your favorite worship song, take your Bible with you, and eat and drink and feast at the King's table. He has been waiting for you. He cannot wait for you to experience His goodness…

Prayer:

Heavenly Father,

I thank You for wanting to spend time with me; I thank You for the wonderful things You have prepared for me at Your table. I ask You to forgive me for feeding on other things, things that have driven me away from You. I ask You for the gift of hunger. I ask You to draw me to You, just as Your Son, Jesus spoke about in John 6:44. I want to sit at Your table, I want to dine with You, I want to taste Your goodness!

In Jesus' name, Amen.

LOVE

"There is no fear in love..."

SHE RESTED HER *head on His massive shoulders. The girl initially ran to her Father in pain, and desperation, yet now as she rested, the reason why she sought Him had all but left her. There she felt safe, nothing mattered and all that was wrong within her world was muted to a perfect stillness. Safe. Nothing could hurt her. There was nothing to be afraid of. The warmth of His love radiated all around her and that brought her to a knowing of absolute safety. She could close her eyes, rest and know that her Father, this massive Force of Love that surrounded her was not about to let anything touch her.*

The Word of God places a high priority upon love. And with good reason, love is the very character of God. It is the essence of who He is. It is because of love that God sent His son Jesus to save us. Love endured stripes so that we could be healed. It is because of Love that He makes provision for us, it is love that delivers us, it is love that keeps us safe, and out of this deep love come the most profound prophetic words that drip with promise for a beautiful future. Love.

Many wonder what the greatest weapon against the enemy is. Is it prayer? Is it fasting? Is it speaking in tongues? I truly believe it is love. When you release love into a situation, real love, agape love,

love that covers a multitude of sin kind of love—you are releasing God Himself into a situation...and when you release God into a situation, beloved reader, there is no telling what can happen!

It is impossible to address God's love without also addressing its adversary, contrary to popular belief, love's rival isn't hate, but it is actually fear. 1 John 4:18 (KJV) tells us, "...perfect love casteth out fear..." Everything you and I will do, everything we see, everything we hear, every decision we make will either be filtered through fear or through love. Think about the last thing you responded to today. The letter in the mail that shows your phone bill skyrocketed, and you're not sure how you are going to pay it. Will you respond out of fear? Wondering how you are going to make it this month? Will you wonder how you are going to communicate without a phone... or will that phone bill, that letter in the mail be filtered through love? When we have the certainty that we have an Almighty God that loves us and happens to not only be our Father but also our Provider, we can confidently trust that because He loves us, He will take care of us.

Love and fear are the two defining elements in a person's life. We are either controlled by love or by fear. If we see the hand of God, the good in situations we face, as difficult as they may be, we are controlled by love. However, if all we see is the hand of darkness, our outlook being bleak and negative in our daily living, we are allowing ourselves to be controlled by fear.

Something our Heavenly Father has instructed, commanded us even, is to NOT give into fear! Numerous times in the Word of God we are told, "...Do not fear..."

Isaiah 41:10 tells us not fear because God is with us; not to be dismayed, because He is our God. God will strengthen, help us and uphold us with His righteous right hand!

The psalmist told us what to do when fear wants to creep its way into our lives, "When I am afraid, I put my trust in you." Psalm 56:3(NIV) And the Apostle Paul tells us in his letter to the people in Philippi, "... not to be anxious about anything..." Philippians 4:6-7

These are just a few reminders on what we are to do with the matter of fear.

So, why is it that we must be reminded continuously not to fear? Our loving Father, warns us through these scriptures of the number one tactic our enemy, the devil, will use against us—fear. When we give into fear, we are essentially agreeing with our enemy. I hardly think anyone in their right mind would vocalize the following statements, "You're right Satan, my son is nothing but a loser, and he is probably going to remain in drug addiction all his life and will more than likely end up dead in an alley somewhere." "I agree with you, devil, I am going to end up penniless and will probably end up living in a cardboard box after I'm evicted from my home." "You're right, Satan, I will never enter into my purpose or fulfill my calling; You're right, Satan, I will never overcome—I will always fail and never conquer." We may not voice it, yet the spirit realm hears us loud and clear. The enemy makes it such a priority to promote fear in our lives—because it paralyzes us and dislocates us from our purpose.

I find Isaiah 51:12-16 (NIV) very interesting:

"I, even I, am he who comforts you.
Who are you that you fear mere mortals, human beings who
are but grass, that you forget the Lord your Maker, who
stretches out the heavens and who lays the foundations of
the earth, that you live in constant terror every day because
of the wrath of the oppressor, who is bent on destruction?
For where is the wrath of the oppressor?
The cowering prisoners will soon be set free; they will
not die in their dungeon, nor will they lack bread.
For I am the Lord your God, who stirs up the sea so that
its waves roar— the Lord Almighty is his name.
I have put my words in your mouth and cov-
ered you with the shadow of my hand—

I who set the heavens in place, who laid the foundations
of the earth, and who say to Zion, 'You are my people."

God is dealing with a fearful people here. The words He speaks
are more of a reproof instead of an assurance. Yet in times when
we are trembling with fear and our imagination has gone wild, God
does not come in with a soothing voice telling us, "Oh sweetheart, it's
ok, don't you worry, I'll take care of everything." The words He spoke
in Isaiah were those of a mighty Father telling His children, "Hey get
it together! I am the one that comforts you! Have you not noticed My
size? Who do you think you are being afraid?"

When fear strikes us, we tend to make it more about us, and God
asks us, "Since when did it become about you and stop being about
Me?" We sometimes very much need a wakeup call like that—a
wakeup call that isn't sympathetic to the fear we have embraced but
rather allows us to realize that when we choose fear we are choosing
the inferior instead of choosing the Absolute God that will take care
of us.

Isaiah tells us of a powerful truth, in chapter 54, verse 13, "…You
shall be far from oppression, for you shall not fear…" Every time we
deny fear an entrance into our hearts and minds, we immediately
quench any oppression that wants to tag along with it.

An oppression is much like a cloud of darkness that makes
its way into our lives the moment we make an agreement with a
lie whereby we invite the atmosphere of darkness to influence our
thoughts and values. The purpose of fear is to mess us up, to connect
us to a lie and later kill us.

Beloved reader, what are you doing with the issue of fear? Have
you been entertaining negative thoughts that cause you to be fearful,
weak and anxious? Have you been losing sleep because of the non-
sense you have been meditating on?

The good news is you know how to *meditate*—so now you
need to change the subject of what you have been focusing on. Stop

feeding your mind and heart on that which will kill you and start feeding on what will bring you life! It really is a choice—that's all it is.

How does perfect love cast out all fear? We have, for many years, been taught that we have to make sure we are in a place of receiving love from God because that love will cast out all fear—and that's partially true. There is more to it, however. The word "*perfect*" means complete. Complete love. Love that is made complete. This love is made complete when I give away what I have received—*that is the kind of love that casts out fear.*

I feel my spirit leap as I share this with you, precious man and woman of God! Because this is the kind of stuff that will cause a revolution in your life, your home, your church and territory! It is not just my experience through prayer that causes love to be perfected in me, it is the experience that I have had with God that is translated in *how I treat people.*

What do we do when fear comes knocking at our door trying to terrorize us? Our heavenly Father tells us to start serving someone, we must stop waiting for the sympathy of others and look to others and serve them. When we are in the middle of a fearsome trial all we want is out—yet our deliverance begins when we are no longer concerned with the size of our problem. You may be thinking, "You have no idea what I've been through." That's fair and true enough, I don't know what you have been through but let's not stay stuck on what we have all been through, let's make our way out—and the way to get out is by serving someone who is more than likely worse off than you.

Love must be practical where it is demonstrated. 1 John 4:18-21 (NIV) says,

> There is no fear in love. But perfect love drives out
> fear, because fear has to do with punishment. The
> one who fears is not made perfect in love.

We love because he first loved us. *Whoever claims to love God yet hates a brother or sister is a liar. For whoever does not love their brother and sister, whom they have seen, cannot love God, whom they have not seen. And he has given us this command: Anyone who loves God must also love their brother and sister.* (emphasis mine)

Can you imagine what our lives and cities would look like if we allowed love to be perfected in us?

I recall some time ago, I was experiencing perhaps one of the most difficult times in my life. I felt so rejected, so alone…so misunderstood. I went to my favorite place, to meet with my Father. I felt His love being deposited in me so strong. It really is in those moments that nothing else matters. It was while I felt His love wrap around me so strongly that I got the impression to give gifts to those that I had hurt—mind you these individuals had nothing to do with what I was experiencing at the time. The Lord reminded me of these people and I simply obeyed. I mentioned this at the beginning and I will mention it again, because it is something that must be carved into our very hearts—Love is the character of God.

Oftentimes when there has been hurt or rejection we close ourselves up to love and to be loved. Pastor Erica Soto shares her testimony:

I suppose you can say that my life was very unexpected. My mother found out she was pregnant with her sixth child at the age of 42. Doctors warned her about the risks of having a less than perfect baby because of her age. There were quite a few family members that readily suggested an abortion. My mother refused.

During her pregnancy, she was invited by a neighbor to a home Bible study. When she got to the Bible study, my mother began to cry because she felt something she had never felt before—the tangible presence of God. She gave her life to God, despite my father's opposition to her new faith in God, she continued going to the Bible studies and growing in God.

It was evident that God's hand was upon me—everything that was said that was going to be wrong with me—was not. I was my parents' miracle baby. There were huge expectations for my life and for what God had planned for me. I felt such a responsibility to overachieve because of this. I felt such pressure to perform. I was after all the miracle baby, the reason why my entire family came to know Jesus. In grade school, I always earned very high marks. I was all business, even as a child when it came to my performance—and my parents and older siblings were too—in fact I remember the shock they expressed when I had given them an average performance on a test I took as a first grader. It's funny now, but I know that moment marked me. I continued on in middle school—excellence was what I was after. One teacher, I remember, asked my parents if I was mute. I wouldn't speak to anyone, I just went to school and turned in the very best work I could. In high school, I was in every club possible, cheerleading, National Honor Society, graduated top ten of my class and every summer during my college years I spent in Galveston's medical school. I was going somewhere.

Although I had been raised in the Christian faith, during my high school and college years, I was not at all committed to God. I was committed to myself. It was all about me. Even after I had recommitted my life to God, I was still very much bound by rejection. My desire to excel in everything found its way into ministry too. As a worship leader, although in my work all the t's were crossed and all the i's were dotted, there was still that issue of rejection. I married a wonderful man, yet the rejection was still there. God blessed me with a baby...and the rejection wouldn't budge, which blocked any flow of love to or from me.

I couldn't understand why I felt rejected, I couldn't understand why my work in the ministry felt as if it were suddenly coming to an abrupt stop during my pregnancy, in a time where I thought everything was supposed to be joyous and beautiful. Even as I tried to breastfeed my baby boy, I saw rejection manifest when he refused to be breastfed.

I cannot say that it was one specific moment that delivered me from rejection and caused me to all of a sudden walk in the perfect love of God. As a worshipper, I had many beautiful encounters with His love; yet love became perfected in my life when I removed the attention off myself and I began to share the love and compassion that God had poured into me. This has become an everyday thing for me. My son is 17 months old now, God has a way of revealing His beautiful uncon-ditional love through the relationship I have with my little one. I no longer am focused on what people will say or think if I don't perform. I have taken the focus off of myself and I have chosen to give others the love that God has so generously and freely poured on me.

When Ignite Movement first opened its doors in 2012, God had given my husband and me specific instructions. Love was to be the main ingredient in our church. Love is the character of God—He wanted His character to be in every detail of Ignite. God tells us the reason why love must be in every detail of our lives, homes and churches in 1 Corinthians 13. In this scripture, He pretty much tells us—You can be the best of the best, have the best choir, have the best musicians, have the most beautiful sanctuary—but if My character isn't in it, if love isn't in it then you don't gain a single thing.

Have you ever been jealous? That's not love. Do you have a tendency to always look out for #1? That's not love. Is there pride, offense, are you critical of others or even rude? That is not love. Love will always be attacked because it is so powerful. Love makes you and me powerful. Genuine love is something the enemy hates, because every time he sees love, he sees God and is reminded of his defeat. It was love after all that defeated him.

Beloved we cannot afford to give fear any kind of hold over our lives. Fear does not care who you are, how powerfully you are used, how prophetic you are or how many souls you have won. As a matter of fact, the spirit of fear watches for any opportunity it can ambush you. The prophet Elijah is a perfect example of this. The book of 1 Kings, chapters 18 and 19 depict how a spirit of fear can dramatically affect an individual. We learn how Elijah boldly confronts not only the people of Israel that had turned to idolatry but also the 400 false prophets of Asherah. Elijah calls fire from heaven and God did not disappoint—fire fell. In holy indignation, he went on to kill all 400 of these prophets that sat to eat at Jezebel's table. "Now therefore send, and gather to me all Israel unto mount Carmel, and the prophets of Baal four hundred and fifty, and the prophets of the groves four hundred, which eat at Jezebel's table." (1 Kings 18:19 KJV)

That very day an idolatrous people repented and turned back to worship the one true God. Not everyone rejoiced, however, there was a very wicked queen, Jezebel that was out for blood. She threatened to kill Elijah the very same way he killed her prophets. Jezebel's words were so toxic, that Elijah went from experiencing the exhilarating rush of glorious victory to trembling in fear and wishing he could hide somewhere and die.

What Elijah the prophet experienced may have been thousands of years ago, but it is that same Jezebelic spirit that comes to attack love. This spirit caused the prophet to want to go into hiding, fearful, depressed with not an ounce of faith left in him. Yet just one chapter before, we read how this man's faith called fire from heaven! Elijah was no longer walking in faith. He fled in fear and wanted to die, no longer loving or valuing his own life, no longer bold in faith. Elijah was afraid and ran for his life. (1 Kings 19:3)

Faith and love walk together, Jezebel had purposed to snuff both out.

When we no longer walk in faith or love, our hearts harden. We read in Pastor Erica's testimony that rejection and fear of rejection had hardened her heart. There are so many things that can harden our hearts, disappointments, failure, unanswered prayers, offense and unforgiveness just to name a few.

Our ability to love and be perfected in love has so much to do with our maturity. As a matter of fact, our maturity is based on our love gauge. Do we still love others in the middle of a crisis? Do we rejoice in a genuine sense of love when others get the very same answer to a prayer that we have been waiting for? Do we still "love others deeply," as 1 Peter 4:8 says and forgive them regardless of the offense allowing for love to cover a multitude of sins? I have made a marked decision in my life. You can offend me, you can hurt me, talk bad about me—but I will still love you.

Love is the wonderful glue that brings us and keeps us closely knit together as the Body of Christ. There is no division in love. The quickest and surest way to kick out any division in our families, homes, church is to love. Love deeply, love genuinely, love like our beautiful Savior demonstrated for us—to love the offender, love the outcast, love the sinner, love the unlovely, love...

When we experience this perfected love in our lives, it transforms us. There is no way a man or woman that experiences deposits of God's love on a daily basis and then turns around and pours God's love on those that surround them can have low self-esteem. Because in those moments with our Father we can perceive just how precious we are to Him and as we lean our heads to His chest we can hear how His heart beats for all of humanity. Being partakers of Heaven's eternal love changes the way we see ourselves.

Beloved Bride of Christ—the Bridegroom will soon return! Scriptures teach us that He is coming for a bride. His bride, not a church but His Bride. Just as a bride prepares for her wedding and looks for the perfect dress; a dress that takes months to make, adding the beautiful detail, the beads, the intricate embroidery willing to spend all kinds of money on this dress she will wear only one day. But that day, there will be no other day like it, and she will remember it for years to come...there is an alarm within me! My prayer is that you are awakened to be that Bride that prepares herself—whether you are a man or woman—prepare yourself for the Bridegroom, Jesus. He is returning for a bride that has taken the time to mature and grow in love, in His love, and make herself ready. A wedding that will outdo every wedding that has ever taken place on the face of this earth is soon to take place. Bride get ready! Just as any bride enjoys the privileges of being joined to her bridegroom, his name becomes her name, his wealth becomes her wealth—so shall it be with this glorious wedding that will soon take place. The Mighty One of Israel, the Omnipotent God is about to place the biggest ring around our finger telling us, *My beautiful Bride, you are Mine...and everything that's Mine is now yours...*

Yet we must get ready, we must mature in love, we must die and seek wholeheartedly what pleases our bridegroom and then do it. I have been married to my amazing husband for over 24 years. In these 24 years, I have purposed myself to know what Andy likes and what he doesn't, because I love him and I want to please him. My husband is a man's man—he does not do chick flicks. Early on in our marriage, when we cuddled on the couch for a movie night, I learned to die to myself and sit through numerous John Wayne westerns. Westerns are not my favorite—in fact I still don't like westerns, but when my husband wants to watch a movie with me, I will sit next to him and watch it, because that's what he enjoys.

What a privilege to be called the Bride of Christ! Beloved reader, please consider this, a bride is loved, cherished and desired. A bride and bridegroom have a passionate desire to be together for all time, they are in an intimate and exclusive relationship. There is no relationship more passionate or fulfilling than the one God offers us—no relationship compares to His.

I am in a passionate and loving relationship with God. He loves me and I love Him, and it is this love that causes me to obey—on command, on request, on whatever. I obey Him because I love Him—that's relationship. I am not a fearful slave to obey out of law or out of fear of punishment—no, I do what my Beloved asks of me because I am so passionately in love with Him. I obey to please Him out of my love for Him.

Almighty God is stretching His hand out to you today precious man or woman. He invites you to experience His love. A love that is so complete, a love that drives out all fear, a love so contagious it compels us to love others, a love that will join us to Him for all of eternity.

Say this prayer so that the perfect love of God can be activated in you today:

Heavenly Father,

I ask you to forgive me for walking in fear. I repent from all fear, disobedience, sin, hard-heartedness and rejection in my life. I don't want any of it in me! I want to know You, I want to know Your love. Your love that is perfected in me so that I can pour out on others the perfect, unconditional love that You have poured out on me. Father fill me with your love.

In Jesus' name. Amen.

PLEASING THE KING

SHE STUDIED THE tiny details of the men's watch in her hand for what seemed to be hours. He wasn't a man that had many favorites of anything. He was generally easy to please and what seemingly pleased him was to see her happy for he loved her deeply. That's why she never forgot the conversation when he mentioned how he would love to one day own a watch like this. He had been so kind to her, so loving, he had given her so much.

The jewelry attendant breathed heavily, reminding her where she was at. She looked up and smiled, "The question isn't whether or not I will purchase here today, sir." She glanced back at the fine piece of jewelry in her hand. "My struggle is whether or not this will be enough..." She wanted to give him everything in the whole store if she could, she wanted to give him everything...period. She was so in love with him. She couldn't wait to see him smile, she couldn't wait to see the look on his face as he opened up the small box tonight. She loved to please him. She loved to make him happy. She loved him...

Throughout the scriptures we find incredible generals and warriors such as Joshua, one of the greatest military leaders that led the people of Israel into the Promised Land. We also have Joseph, a man that in spite of suffering accusation and persecution, rose to be Egypt's second in command and wisely preserved a people that surely would have perished in the seven-year famine. And then there is David. The man that killed lions, bears and giants *before* becoming king of Israel. These are just a few of the mighty men that we read about in the pages of the Bible. What made these men incredible generals and warriors? What was it that made them so fierce? So militarily brilliant in battle?

One strong characteristic we see in these men and women was their strong, intense passion to please Almighty God—their King. There is an account in the Bible that I find fascinating. It is found in 2 Samuel 23:15-17 (NIV):

David longed for water and said, "Oh, that someone would get me a drink of water from the well near the gate of Bethlehem!" [16] So the three mighty warriors broke through the Philistine lines, drew water from the well near the gate of Bethlehem and carried it back to David. But he refused to drink it; instead, he poured it out before the Lord. [17] "Far be it from me, Lord, to do this!" he said. "Is it not the blood of men who went at the risk of their lives?" And David would not drink it. Such were the exploits of the three mighty warriors.

David's request for a drink of water wasn't as simple as it sounded. It was a difficult task; he didn't want just any drink of water—he wanted it from a special well near the gate of Bethlehem. The Good News Translation says David was homesick and was longing for a drink of water from that particular well. Was it a life or death situation? Did David have to have a drink of water from that place? No. A drink of water from that well simply would have pleased him.

There was one thing, however, the well was behind enemy lines and it was infested with Philistine enemies. To retrieve this kind of drink for the king could prove to be very dangerous, deadly even. It would not be an easy task to bring back a refreshing drink for the king.

These three mighty warriors loved David deeply. Therefore, no request was too great when it came to the commander that believed in them and trained them in a dark cave full of distressed, bitter and indebted men. "David left Gath and escaped to the cave of Adullam. When his brothers and his father's household heard about it, they went down to him there. ² All those who were in distress or in debt or discontented gathered around him, and he became their commander. About four hundred men were with him." (1 Samuel 22:1-2 NIV)

They cared very much about their king and commander that they were willing to sacrifice their lives to please him. I imagine that when they heard that their king longed for this drink, all they wanted to do was to be able to fulfill his desire and answer his request to bring him the very thing that would give him pleasure.

I am certain that they considered the cost required of them: their time, their effort, their lives even. Yet they would not let that keep them from immediately responding, without hesitation, to David's desire. They responded in such a way that they did not give it a second thought; they did not question it, ponder on it or reason it; because their desire to give the king what he wanted was so deep.

*That is what love does—it pushes you, impulses you to **do**.*

This is something we should all strive for in our lives, that we would have that same love for our King and Commander, Jesus Christ. To be one who leaps to answer the simplest or most seemingly impossible request that comes from our Savior's lips. I want to be one who would do anything, go anywhere, and give everything for the sake of bringing Him pleasure and responding to any desire of His heart. I want to answer His request, without hesitation, no matter the cost—to my time, energy, reputation, bank account, or even my life—simply because I love Him; simply because He is beautiful and wonderful and deserving of it; simply because He is my King.

The desire to please the king was greater than any fear that these three men would face. When we have a passion to please the King we will take risks and overcome obstacles, hurdle any situation and overcome the greatest opposition.

Where does the desire to please God come from? The desire to please God comes from *loving* Him. It's really no big secret, when you love Him you want to please Him. Jesus said in John 8:29, "And he that sent me is with me: the Father hath not left me alone; for I do always those things that please him."

Ephesians 5:10 tells us try to discern what is pleasing to the Lord. When you love someone, you want to please them. When you love someone, you are willing to go through anything to make them smile. You're willing to learn their language, learn to make their favorite dish, wear your hair the way they like it, learn a hobby to be near them... Go to the mall and shop for hours—do I hear the men say an "amen"?

Beloved reader, our love for God must be passionate, strong, alive and deep. Many people have lost their love for God—that's why the desire to please God has left them only to find that they are only pleasing themselves just as 2 Timothy states, "many will be lovers of their own selves..."

Precious Bride, we must go back and be restored to loving our King!

Love, I believe, has been robbed from us. One of Satan's strategies is to kill, to murder, to strip and turn off the Agape love of God. Satan does not know love—he has no love.

Love is the remedy for fear;
Love is the remedy for unforgiveness;
Love is the remedy for insecurity;
Love is the remedy for rejection...
Love is the perfect antidote for all that is not of God.
That is why 1 Corinthians 13:13 (NIV) says, "...And now these three remain: faith, hope and love. But the greatest of these is love."

Why is love the greatest? No other attribute has been the perfect embodiment of God other than love. Love truly never fails. It cannot. When we release love into a situation, any situation—it doesn't matter how ugly it may be—we *release God* into a situation and God, beloved, God never fails.

Satan's assignment is to stir up and cook up anything; any problem, situation, circumstance, disagreement, annoyance or thought to separate us from that love, to kill the Agape love of God.

Love, today, has become superficial; not real; not deep; but rather fake, not genuine— too many people jealous of one another or offended or have a hard heart— and that is not the Agape Godly love. Throughout the years, I have encountered people with a hardened heart, I have come across people who cannot even return a hug when they are being hugged.

Just as any parent is pleased to see their children get along, whether sharing a toy as toddlers or keeping the peace as adults—it pleases the Father to see His children get along.

I believe as we seek God's presence, our love is refreshed, it is rekindled and deepened. One cannot possibly come to God and not melt in His presence. Yet, this is the goal of the enemy—to separate us from this power producing relationship we are invited to have with God.

When we love God there is a response and we are willing to surrender anything—relationships, careers, money, time, our own desires—anything. When we love God deeply we live our lives searching and longing to find out what pleases the KING.

Pastor Flor Lopez shares her testimony on some of the choices she has made because of her deep desire to please God:

From my earliest years, I remember God has always been a part of my life, so to me, wanting to have a relationship with Him was very natural. When my friends would play, they would want to pretend they were a doctor or teacher--I would play church. I remember setting up our "church" outside of the apartments where I used to live. My brothers and I would find household items in order to try to create a church environment. We would line up chairs for the congregation, one of my brothers would use buckets turned upside down and sticks to play drums. Another brother would help the imaginary congregation to their seats, while yet another brother would preach.

Church was very much a part of our lives. My mother would line all four of my siblings and me up and we would make the often long, hot walk to our church on Sundays. As a child, I would always find myself praying. Hearing the sound of ambulance or firetruck sirens would always prompt me to for those that might have been in trouble or in some kind of accident. I also remember praying for the well-being of my family and for our family's business.

In elementary school, I was always talking to people about God, people often sought me for comfort and peace. Sure, I played with dolls and had friends, but I was certain that my life was set apart for God because I had supernatural encounters with God from a very young age. I experienced healing in my eyes and received 20/20 vision—doctors were puzzled upon examining my eyes, they could not explain the sudden and supernatural occurrence. There were days as a little girl, in which because of the presence of God all I did was weep and I even remember experiencing the manifestations of gold dust...God was so much a part of me. There was no question when it came to the will of God in my life, my desire was to do whatever I felt He wanted me to do.

At the age of 14, I began to attend a youth group, where at the time, Apostle Patty was the youth leader. I immediately felt connected to the love and passion for God that was so evident there. There have been two major passions in my life—God and sports, yet when I began to attend the youth groups, I had such a hunger for more of God and what I would experience there, that I would quickly leave my volleyball practices and rush off to church in search of more of God.

There was something very different that was happening in my young life—in all my childhood I saw God's attributes, manifestations, and His goodness but I never knew Him. My image of God had been contained in a box, yet, when I got to Ignite Movement it opened up my spiritual eyes and guided me towards Him, towards a deep and intimate relationship with Almighty God. These were not your typical youth services I was attending. It was definitely not hotdog night there! We were being ushered into a deeper walk with the living God. Although I had experienced God before as a little girl, I never knew what it was to love Him. I fell so deeply in love with God and I was so consumed in knowing Him and doing His will. I was so passionate to please Him— yes, even as a teenager, my passion was to please God.

I later entered into a relationship with a guy that was part of the same youth group. Everything seemed perfect, we were both leaders, seemingly working together for God. I was with him for four years and about to get married to him, when I realized that this relationship was not in the will of God. —I feel that there is a young woman, you are in a relationship with someone at your church, everyone thinks you all make the perfect couple, but you know that the relationship you are in is not the will of God for your life—

I had other opportunities to get into other relationships, but my pursuit for God has kept me focused and set apart. I have been a witness to others trying to please people, and at times I have been lured to get into the same—yet deep inside I have always had a conviction that I've been created to please God. My desire has been to bring pleasure to Him. I find delight in His commandments. I know that if all I was created for was to please God that I would be fulfilling my purpose. I have found, that as I please God I have come upon my purpose.

Even through persecution, my desire for God, has always sustained me close to Him. Every sacrifice I have ever made, my time, every sleepless night, giving, surrendering relationships, has always been driven by my love for Him. Even after having a career and a secular job they did not bring fulfillment to my life. It was my pastor, Apostle Patty, that was able to recognize the calling over my life as an intercessor. Through prayer, I have become aware of what pleases God such as winning souls, serving others, standing in the gap, discipling and mentoring others.

Knowing the will of God and doing it, has caused me to find purpose and fulfillment in my life. In pleasing God, I have seen the countless *blessings it has brought upon my life. Today, I serve as a pastor at Ignite Movement Church, I also oversee the intercession ministry. I am certain that it was back when I was a little girl wanting to please Him and feeling the need to pray for others at the sound of sirens, that God was setting me apart to serve Him as an end time intercessor.*

Pleasing the King must not be approached as a kid does when it's time to do chores, dragging their feet, dreading the whole ordeal. No! Pleasing our King has great rewards! David's great warriors, the three that risked their lives to bring him a drink of water from that particular well will be remembered throughout all time for that exploit and many others. While pleasing our King may not be easy—it is a discipline that will yield great rewards.

When we love God deeply and want to please Him, we are in search of what pleases the King. I ask God continuously in my prayer closet, "Father what pleases you? What do you want? What do you crave? I just live to please you."

That should be our response daily to the love that He pours on us, because that is what love does. Love gives. When we love someone, we want to please them. Agape love does that to us; it causes us to put our own desires aside for the other person. That is the perfect depiction of the Father's love. He loved the world so much that He gave His only Son (John 3:16). A good indication that the Agape love of God is present is the desire to find out what pleases the other person.

Scripture teaches us what pleases the Father. Here are just a few:

Faith pleases the King "And without faith it is impossible to please God, because anyone who comes to him must believe that he exists and that he rewards those who earnestly seek him."
Hebrews 11:6 (NIV)

Fear of the Lord pleases the King (fear of the Lord is having a reverence and respect for Him)

"He does not delight in the strength of the horse; He takes no pleasure in the legs of a man.

The Lord takes pleasure in those who fear Him, in those who hope in His mercy."
Psalms 147:10-11(NKJV)

Praise pleases the King I will praise the name of God with a song, and will magnify Him with thanksgiving. *This* also shall please the Lord better than an ox *or* bull, which has horns and hooves. Psalms 69:30-31(NKJV)

Keeping His commandments pleases the King "If you love me, keep My commandments." John 14:15 (NIV)

Speaking His words and having His thoughts pleases the King- "May these words of my mouth and this meditation of my heart be pleasing in your sight, LORD, my Rock and my Redeemer." Psalm 19:14 (NIV)
A humble and obedient heart also please the King.

David's mighty men were willing to risk their lives just to please the king. They sacrificed their lives and put themselves in a dangerous situation just to get the king a drink of water. That is deep love. I imagine their love, gratitude and devotion to David was so profound. No request was too great.

"You want a drink from that well my king? Done."

How could they not respond in such a way? How could they not be grateful to a commander that saw past their weakness, their flaws and trained them to be fierce warriors? Fierce enough to singlehandedly defeat hundreds?
Beloved, how could we not respond with the same zeal, passion and devotion when it comes to pleasing our King? He has lovingly seen past our many flaws, our weaknesses. We too at some time

or another have been in a dark cave of despair and distress. Bitter because of life's circumstances. Yet, our skilled Commander knows exactly what it will take to pull a warrior out of us. How could we not respond with an absolute desire to please our King?

> *"You want me to believe You my King? You want me to honor and obey You? You want me to forgive? You want me to praise You, keep Your commands and have the right thoughts? Your thoughts? I don't care how many enemies I have to go through to do it, but consider it done…"*

Mighty warrior of God, say this prayer with me:

Father,

I ask you to please forgive me for looking after only what pleases me. I repent. My desire is to please You. I want You to smile with every choice and decision I make in my life. I ask that You would give me Your grace to be able to please you every moment of every day of my life.

In Jesus' name. Amen!

POOR IN SPIRIT

A few words on being poor...

THE YOUNG BUSINESSMAN *turned from side to side on his bed, trying to find a comfortable spot. It had been a long day. Thoughts of all he had to do with his business, the powerful oil empire he had inherited from his late father—would not leave him—he was on the verge of the biggest financial transaction his company would ever know and he didn't want to make a wrong move. Words from the last conversation he had with his wife echoed in, he fluffed his pillow, determined to get some rest. He often felt he was being pulled in a thousand different directions. He wished he had his father so that he could go into the old familiar office and ask him so many questions he needed answers to. Sighing deeply, the much sought-after sleep finally came...*

The young man looked around, he didn't understand what he was doing in his father's old office nor could he see who sat behind his father's desk.

"Tell Me, son, what do you want?" The voice was gentle, kind, yet very strong. His heart beat wildly, he had so much to ask for; he had so many questions. He needed so much help. Even before all the questions he had intended to ask formed in his mind, the young man

immediately answered, "I need Your help; I don't know what to do. Give me wisdom," he answered pleadingly.

We are so often intrigued with the success of others. We ask questions like, "How did they do that?" And, "How did they get there?" We are, in fact, so curious that even lists like the Forbes 400 exist for our perusal; they tell us the person's net worth, their age (for those of us who think maybe time is running out) and what it is that made them all that money.

At times, we look at someone's profile and associate their success to their skill, intelligence or perseverance even. In the Kingdom of God, that is not always the case. Especially when we take a close look at the lives of the most powerful men mentioned in the Word of God.

David was a gifted musician, a prolific psalmist, a sagacious king, he was strategical at war and highly apt in physical combat. Yet, when David thought of himself, his attitude was along the lines of—*I don't involve myself in complicated matters...*

> *"Lord, my heart is not haughty,*
> *Nor my eyes lofty.*
> *Neither do I concern myself with great matters,*
> *Nor with things too profound for me."* Psalm 131:1 (NKJV)

David, the most powerful man on the planet, having unbelievable capacity to conquer enemies, wrote of himself, "I don't think I'm better than others nor do I get involved with complicated matters." His strength was not in human devotion, nor was it found in human discipline, although both have value.

David's strength came from his utter dependence on God. This shepherd turned king was quite aware that his human strength would fail him, he knew he was incapable of fulfilling the many tasks set before him. I could almost hear the breathless, bewildered shepherd shout victoriously after having killed a lion and a bear, "That was so God!" David knew that this *Super-Power* to defeat lions, bears, giants and 10,000's came directly from God almighty.

This dependence on God ran in the family. There is a story in 1 Kings 3. It tells us about Solomon, the son of David. Solomon was now king, and had the weight of leading the people of Israel. While Solomon slept, Almighty God showed up in his dreams. God tells Solomon, "Ask of Me whatever you want and I will give it to you!"

It is amazing enough that God would show up in a dream and say, "Ask me whatever you want, I'll give it to you." Yet, I believe that something extraordinary is overlooked. We have read this story many times and have failed to see the magnificence in Solomon's response. Many of us would have answered in the response for the immediate, for the now, "God I need $500 to pay my rent this month." "I need a car, God!" "I'm so lonely, God! I want my future mate!"

Solomon's response, however, was an honorable one. How is it that an individual can be so trained for purpose that God can show up in your dreams and trust you to make such an important decision while you are sound asleep? Many people would be dumbfounded if God were to ask them this very question while being wide awake! But Solomon's answer was so purposed and intentional that it pleased God.

Solomon answered God by pleading for wisdom. Solomon was actually asking for a hearing ear, because this is actually what gives us wisdom. It is a hearing from another world, and he knew that if he did not hear God, he would not be able to lead the people of Israel. He desperately needed to hear God's instructions! The new king of Israel was so filled with purpose that while he *slept* God was able to ask him such a crucial question. A question that would ultimately affect a nation. This new king had been groomed since childhood for the great responsibility to lead Israel.

The story in 1 Kings 3, depicts just how humble, how dependent and how *real* before God Solomon was. This new king did not sit on the throne with an immediate task list of what was to be done. He needed God's help. He tells God, "I'm a child, I don't know how to do what You assigned me to do, I don't have the ability or the capacity to do this." (Paraphrased)

Needless to say, God's heart was delighted with Solomon's response. He could have asked God for anything—*anything*. But instead he asked for help, for a hearing ear to lead God's people. God told him, Solomon, "because you did not ask me for wealth, for a long life or the destruction of your enemies I will give you the hearing ear you asked for and everything else anyway."

This sounds very similar to something that Jesus would say hundreds of years later, in Matthew 6:33 (NKJV) " But seek first the kingdom of God, and his righteousness; and all these things shall be added to you." There is something that happens to us when our priorities are right. There is a trickle effect of inevitable blessings that come on us. Things that we are not chasing after, because we are in pursuit of Kingdom things, those things chase and overtake us.

I don't know about you, but I would have loved to have been one of the many in the multitude listening to Jesus' famous Sermon on the Mount. The first beatitude He began with was "Blessed are the poor in spirit..." Matthew 5:3 (KJV)

There are many misconceptions about being poor in spirit. When we think of the word "poor" or someone who is poor and we automatically think of someone who is needy. Beloved reader, being needy is not always a bad thing. Not when it comes to being poor in spirit. To be poor in spirit, however, is not finding oneself in a place of self-criticism, self-beating, or self-rejection, and much less false humility— those are all counterfeit.

A person that is poor in spirit is one that has complete and total dependency on God. They are *needy* of God. They are aware of their weakness and know they cannot do anything without God. A person that is poor in spirit is one who takes risks because their lives are completely dependent upon God. Their entire life is one that shouts, *"God you gotta show up! Because I can't do it without You! I need You in every area of my life!"*

It is evident when a person is poor in spirit. They take great risks, they are not fearful.

Jesus shared many other beatitudes, he spoke about the merciful, saying that those would obtain mercy, the peacemakers would be called children of God…that's really good stuff—we all need mercy and what a privilege to be called a child of God! But what do the poor in spirit obtain?

The poor in spirit obtain the Kingdom of Heaven. That's right, beloved! You get the *whole* Kingdom. Perhaps some of you have had the erroneous idea that we get the Kingdom of Heaven after we die. It is very possible dear man, dear woman to experience the Kingdom of Heaven here on earth. When one is poor in spirit, access to the entire heavenly realm is obtained, that is to say everything that is available in heaven is made very much available to you, right here on earth: peace, joy, prosperity, health, healing, rest, wealth, victory, fullness, deliverance and so much more —it is not just a taste of the Kingdom, this is all inclusive.

David was poor in spirit. That is what made him great.

Being poor in spirit is what caused God to go into Solomon's bedroom and trust the fairly new and inexperienced king with anything and everything. I imagine that Solomon was quite aware of his need for divine wisdom before God visited his dreams.

It is what Jesus carried. Jesus while on this earth was the epitome of being poor in spirit, because His dependency was on God; He was constantly leaning on His Father.

When we are not poor in spirit we can miss things—important things, opportunities and encounters that can change our lives. In the gospels, we learn about well-trained students of the Word. Perhaps their focus was so intent on the words written in the scrolls that they completely missed the *Word made Flesh* standing in front of them.

Those that are poor in spirit have a hearing ear. They want to listen to God's direction— *they are desperately aware that they need to listen to God's direction.*

Have you ever found yourself talking to a person, giving them advice, counseling them in a certain area of their lives? And as you are pointing things out that perhaps need change so that there may be improvement in their lives—all that is coming out of their mouths is "I know, I know, I know..." I am certain God has experienced that with us plenty of times when we are not poor in spirit. We may not arrogantly tell God, "I know, I know, I know" but our lives and attitudes shout it at Him when we skim through His Word, thinking "read that one before; I know what that Psalm says..." yet there is no true leaning on His Word, and much less obedience.

If you consider yourself a student of the Word, of the scriptures— you better have an ear. Knowing the scripture, having it written in our minds and hearts is good, but a listening ear is what is needed.

Many of us fall into the trap of thinking that we know what God is going to do next, how He will show up next in our lives. If there is something that I have learned throughout the years in my walk with God is that although He is holy, He is not religious; and although He is so steadfast and never changing, He is never boring or predictable.

The scribes, Sadducees and Pharisees were keenly trained in scripture yet they completely missed Jesus when He showed up. The Bible, in Luke chapter 7:36-48, tells us of an individual that perhaps was not so trained in the scriptures, yet she knew exactly who Jesus was when she laid eyes on Him. I imagine this woman took one look at Jesus, approached Him with eyes downcast, despite her feeling unworthy, dirty, despite her past, but because she recognized who He was, worship broke out of her entire being. This woman who lived a sinful life found out that Jesus was eating at the Pharisee's house, so she took her alabaster jar of perfume. She was so moved that her teardrops fell on Jesus' feet. Then she wiped his feet with her hair, kissed them and poured perfume on them. (Luke 7: 37-38) She needed Jesus! This woman probably felt drained, tired of her lifestyle and sin. She needed a change, she needed transformation…she was well aware of her need for Jesus…she was *poor in spirit.*

The Pharisee in this story on the other hand, really did not understand his own need for Jesus. He thought he was fine. In fact, he questioned Jesus in his mind, wondering why He would allow such a sinful woman to get near Him that way. I am reminded of the scripture in Revelation 3:17 (NKJV), "You say, 'I am rich; I have acquired wealth and do not need a thing.' But you do not realize that you are wretched, pitiful, poor, blind and naked." The Savior of the world showed up to have dinner with this man and he did not know it!

Luke 19 tells us of another individual, Zacchaeus, a chief tax collector. In the days of Jesus, being a tax collector was not a very honorable occupation. A tax collector was almost the equivalent of being a shady individual, a crooked thief! When this man, Zacchaeus, that was small in stature, heard that Jesus was passing by—he did not hesitate, he could care less what others thought of him. He went so far as to climb up a tree just to see take a glimpse of Jesus! There was an urgency within him to take one look at this man named Jesus. Seems to be that all the bad, disreputable people knew who Jesus was, and not only that but they were aware of their desperate need for Him.

It is the awareness of need that positions us to see God do the impossible. Those that are poor in spirit can easily surrender, they are broken, and they receive the move of God. Others that are not poor in spirit, however, sadly do not respond to the move of the Spirit, and they do not receive what God is doing. Sadly, I have seen this happen during services. The presence of God and the move of God are so tangible, so electric in the atmosphere. In the midst of deep worship there will be people weeping, crying out to God in their desperate need for Him, yet on the very next row there can be a stern-faced soul, having a very false sense of security in themselves, not aware that they are so in need of Almighty God.

Jesus understood this, He understood that these scholars, these scribes were not poor in spirit. They were not aware of their dire need for Him, the Savior of the world. He looked at all the religious leaders and said, "Well they don't need a physician..." (Luke 2:17) They did not recognize their need for Jesus; the Healer, so they were not able to value what He had brought to them.

God searches for people that are well *aware* that they have no idea what they are doing. Why? Because it pleases Him to give these type of people the Kingdom. Those that do not pretend to know it all. Those that recognize that if they do not receive help or direction from God they are doomed! God loves to hear a desperate, hungry cry from His sons and daughters!

God is not seeking for people that want to be famous. He is looking for those that are poor in spirit, those that will say, "God, You can do whatever You want in me and through me. I need You!"

You know beloved, it is in the "not knowing," the being clueless, the moments that leave you at a loss, that make us so dependent upon God. I can definitely attest to that.

In the fall of 2012, I found myself standing in the backyard of a church member's home, under a porch, before a handful of people. After faithfully serving my dad as youth pastor for numerous years, I had been asked to leave my father's congregation the day before we were supposed to hold our services. That evening, in late September, I stood before a small, wide-eyed congregation, about to preach a message on God's supernatural power. I really had no idea what I was doing. I had no money for a building—as a matter of fact everyone had been asked to bring their own chair! I had no direction as to where I was going to take the people that were looking to me for direction. Looking back, I am certain that it was my total dependency upon God that got me through that season.

How does one survive a thing like that? By being poor in spirit. How does one lead a people, a congregation while going through their own trauma? By being poor in spirit.

Before I took one step (and it was literally one step) onto that tiny black box that my leaders lovingly prepared for me to step on and preach from—I had already put to rest many of the thoughts, worries, anxieties that could have killed me, killed my purpose.

I stepped onto that tiny platform and preached my heart out. I preached like my life and the lives of those listening depended on it—because it did. I was determined that no soul was going to fall through the cracks in this transition! Almighty God, the One whom I so desperately depended on then, and still rely on now, showed up. People were healed and they were delivered. God's joy was so evident that day! I cannot forget to mention that the tiny backyard congregation made up of mostly youth, college aged students and young families picked up an astounding offering of almost *twelve thousand dollars*!

When we are poor in spirit, God shows up in every area of our lives. When we are humble enough to tell God "I need Your help! I'm absolutely lost without You!" He will not hold it against us, rub it in our face, or ask us why we have not learned to do it on our own. Dear reader, in our weakness He truly does show up strong. "But he said to me, 'My grace is sufficient for you, for my power is made perfect in weakness.' Therefore I will boast all the more gladly about my weaknesses, so that Christ's power may rest on me." 2 Corinthians 12:9 (NKJV)

My need for God is so profound. I need God. I need Him to be a good wife; I need Him to be a good mom; I need Him because I must be a good daughter; I need Him to walk in the calling of an apostle; I need Him! I am so needy of Him, of His presence in my life!

Beloved reader, if you have not depended on God completely now is the time to repent; repent for depending on your own human effort and ability, for depending in the natural.

Pray this prayer with me:

Father,

I ask You to forgive me for depending on my own natural ability, on human strength, for depending on natural solutions, instead of looking to You for supernatural help.

I repent! I don't want to depend on myself any longer, I will depend on You!

Holy Spirit come reignite me; prepare me for a greater weight of your presence, of your glory, of your purpose for my life.

I want to have a yielded heart. A heart that is poor in spirit. I want to be totally dependent upon You. Make me ready to take risks.

One thing I am certain of, beloved reader, being poor in spirit has made me truly rich!

THE PROCESS

THE COOL DUSK air fell on David's skin like a blanket preparing him for nighttime. Nights. He didn't know whether he loved them or dreaded them. All he knew was that the separation from his family was beginning to wear on him. He didn't understand why out of all his brothers, he was the one chosen to look after the sheep. He didn't understand why he was rarely invited to partake in any of the family gatherings—he was in fact often overlooked, forgotten. His eyes scanned the fields. He thought he had seen movement behind the tall bushes. 'If the loneliness doesn't kill me' he thought, 'surely a lion or a bear will...' he laughed, trying to shake off any fear. 'I don't understand, Lord. I don't understand what You are doing...' the young man sighed as he grabbed his lyre. His song rose slowly through the night sky, passing the stars, reaching the One he sang to.

I know, I know, this may be the chapter that you are tempted to skip...right about now you may be wanting to flip through a few of the pages and go on to the last chapter, restoration—yeah, everyone likes that. As a matter of fact, you may not only be wanting to skip the pages of this chapter—you may be going through a process and you have been crying out to God for Him to get you out of it, to help you skip this part of your life.

Dear reader, this loving Father has such great plans for us. He deems it necessary for us to go through processes to prepare us for the next great season in our lives.

If you skip this chapter you will be missing what I would consider the "weights" of this book. The process is what bulks you up in spirit, it makes you strong, it changes you...everything in life requires a process.

The word "process" is defined as being the formation, growth, development and progress of something or someone. It is also defined as something that is subject to a process or treatment, *with the aim of readying for some purpose*, improving, or remedying a condition. (synonym.com)

Although, at first glance, the word process may appear to be painful and laborious, but this much avoided "chapter" in our lives is truly something very necessary. Why? Because the process is what is getting us ready for our purpose!

Pastor JoAnn Velasquez, of Ignite Movement, shares the testimony of her process.

At the age of 18, I came to a place in my life where I was desperately looking for answers. My life was a mess. I was a young, fearful, depressed, alcoholic teen mother of a tiny 2-year-old girl. My relationship with my daughter's dad was nothing at all what I wanted—it was in fact a disaster. What I was looking for was freedom and comfort from all my troubles.

One day, my best friend invited me to Ignite Movement. I was born and raised with a Catholic background. I had no idea what I was getting myself into as I walked into Ignite, but I had this knowing that I just had to be there. Shortly after hearing Apostle Patty preach on the fire of God, I could feel this weight of God fall over me and all I could do was weep not knowing or understanding what was happening. I left everything at the altar—all the pain, fear, depression, addiction...I left it all to God! I had finally found what I was desperately looking for. I had found salvation, freedom, and healing. I was aware that this was the starting point of my new life. God had started a new beautiful work in me and I did not want Him to stop! My process had begun!

Two and a half years after I accepted Jesus into my life, I was still fasting and praying and believing for my husband's salvation. This was one of the toughest times in my life. Praying for his salvation was not an easy task. He managed bars for a living and the lifestyle came right along with his job. He was bound to drugs and steroids and there was constant adultery and emotional abuse. But I knew that God's promise to me was that my family was going to serve the Lord.

As I went through this process of praying for the salvation of my husband, Apostle Patty and Pastor Andy continued to stay by my side and taught me how to pray with perseverance until I saw my breakthrough. Through this process, God started to teach me to trust in Him. God then became my husband, my friend, my comforter, and my Father. As God started to work in me, He also started to work in my husband and eventually came to the feet of Christ!

The process was far from over, as my husband and I grew in the things of God, things began to get exposed that were hidden in my heart. God started to deal with my identity. For as long as I can remember I would battle with a lot of fear, rejection and unforgiveness. God dealt with me in many areas and yet, I continued to seek God. He pulled out the pride, independence, fear and rejection. He began to remove the pain from my earthly father and the pain from my husband that I had carried for many years.

Something beautiful happened though, as God continued to work in me I started to find who I was in Him. I found my identity in God! I then started to walk as a daughter of God being able to operate in the supernatural without any fear. The voice of God began to get louder and clearer in my life and God started to use me.

There was a time that I had the honor of going to a missions trip to Poplar, California with Apostle Patty. I remember that as she preached from the altar she called me out and directed me to pray for a lady that had a rare condition and could not walk. The old me would have been afraid, not knowing who I was in God, doubting that this miracle was going to happen. But because God had set me free, I knew that God could do this miracle and that's exactly what He did! As I began to pray for this lady, she stood up and started walking without her walker. God, once again, showed up! My life, since the first day I found God until now, has forever been changed. After 12 years of being committed and faithful to the process, God and my spiritual parents, promoted me and commissioned me as one of the pastors of Ignite Movement Church. Today, I serve God with my husband, and my now 14-year-old daughter loves and serves God too as well as our three young sons. I am forever grateful for my spiritual parents, Pastor Andy and Apostle Patty that have constantly been by my side, encouraging me to persevere and go through the process.

Again, everything in life requires a process, let's take for example the largest trees in the world, the California Redwood trees. These impressive trees have towering heights of over 300 feet. A *single* tree provides a home for *hundreds* of species and not only that, they are able to withstand earthquakes. These powerful giant trees once were seeds that were sown into the ground—seeds that had to die and then break through ground to see the light of day.

If you are reading beyond the natural, I am certain you are capturing this in your spirit. Even these powerful Redwood trees go through a process...

The season of the process in our lives is crucial. This season, however, is the season in which we can get discouraged and begin to doubt God. We must endure this season, because if we do not endure the process or overcome it then the destiny is never reached.

In life, we go through different processes. About four years ago I underwent what I believe to be the most painful process in my life. I felt abandoned and completely alone—but I did not allow myself the option to quit. If you find yourself in a hard season, don't quit! You cannot quit! Keep going, keep pushing, keep growing because before you know it, you will be breaking through the ground like that tiny little seed and will be able to feel the warmth of the sun shining on your face.

During the most afflicting times of life, during difficult situations, in times of pressure and in times of wilderness is when we begin to see what we are truly made of. The way we behave in the middle of pressure, the way we respond, what we do, what we think in the middle of a process, what we speak in the middle of afflictions demonstrate what's on the inside of us. Many things begin to surface during times of trials and tribulations. I think of a pot of water over a hot stove. When the heat is turned up bubbles begin to come up… things in our lives begin to come up in the middle of our process and perhaps that is when we realize that we are not ready for what we anxiously awaited, for what was prophesied over us. We realize that the process is very necessary and are thankful for it—more than likely not during the process, but afterwards.

We discover many things about ourselves when undergoing a process.

Many people abandon the process, they run from it. Some tend to run when offended, and sadly, many never allow God to finish what He started. They abandon not only the process, but tragically their calling, purpose and destiny. They quit too soon! We must persevere and not quit! Perseverance is a characteristic, a key ingredient to undergo any process. The following chapter will cover perseverance more in depth.

Beloved don't let an offense, hurt, pain or even situations cause you to abort the process.

I realized that I had a lot of fears. I had the fear of not succeeding, the fear of failure, fear of man, fear of rejection…the list does go on…in the midst of my process I even had to confront the fact that I had pride. I needed to renew my mind, because my mind was so consumed with *what was done to me*. I had been wronged. I had been abandoned. I had been wounded. I had been left alone. I was consumed daily with what "I" was going through. I was consumed with how others rejected me, how they lied about me and how painful my situation was. I had questions running through my mind, questions of what was going to happen to me, to the ministry, what was going to become of us. "What did I do to deserve this?" I would constantly ask.

That is the epitome of a victim mentality. When we just focus on ourselves, on what was done to us and are consumed with thoughts of the experiences that caused pain, we are nothing other than victims. And God did not create us to live as victims. We must change the victim mentality that wants to keep us bound to the past—bound to pain, bitterness and unforgiveness.

I remember early one morning, my husband and I were taking our daily run. My physical posture had taken on the pain that I was carrying on the inside of me. I literally had a hunch on my back because of the continual pain I felt on my chest due to my circumstances. (I have found that most women carry emotional pain there—in their chest.) As we jogged, I began to share and vent once again how I felt. How unfair everything was and how difficult all this was for me. My husband abruptly stopped me and said, "Stop talking about it. If you want something to die, then stop feeding it."

Those simple words were perhaps the wisest words anyone has ever spoken to me. That moment was a very huge turning point in my life. I thank my husband who is full of wisdom for setting me straight and challenging me to kill the giant that I so graciously fed every day.

So many times, when we go through troubled seasons, when we go through difficult situations we tend to rehash things in our mind. We tend to keep the hurt alive instead of letting go and letting God heal us and turn the ashes into beauty. (Isaiah 61:3)

What we must remember is that what we are experiencing, what we are going through or enduring, as crazy and nonsensical as it may seem, is part of our process; because God is preparing us for greatness.

In the middle of the problem or trial all we can see are the ashes, all we can see is the mess, the bad, the painful circumstance, the husband that left us, the job that we lost, the business that failed, the child that refuses to serve God, the church member that betrayed us…but we must learn to let go. We must choose to make a conscious decision to let go and allow God to make something beautiful in us that was processed during the most difficult situations.

Perhaps, as you read this book, the Spirit of God is bringing to your remembrance things that you have had a difficult time letting go of. You have not been able to let go of the betrayal, the pain, the hurt, the rejection or abandonment. God cannot turn your situation around until you let go and surrender it to Him.

Beloved, let me remind you again: once we let go, God is able to shape and mold us to prepare us for our callings and purposes.

While many of us may think we are ready, ready for the blessing, ready for the prophetic word to come to pass, ready for the calling, ready to step into our purpose, many times however, the process reveals to us that we really are not.

In the middle of my process, I realized I needed so much maturing.

The holidays have always been a special time for my family. Traditionally, my sisters and their families and I gather with our parents. There's the football game to watch after the sharing of the lavish turkey dinner we all often enjoyed. We would laugh and share stories around the table. In our conversations, we would marvel at how fast the year passed us by and talk about our plans for the coming year. My daughters and their cousins laughed and played together…it's a time of family.

In the middle of this very difficult process, naturally, one would think that my family should have been the perfect place of solace, of comfort to hide me away from the pain and rejection I had been experiencing in ministry. This, however, was not the case. The ministry from which I was hurt, and had been asked to leave was not just any ministry—it was my dad's church.

I remember how terribly painful the holidays were. The first Christmas and Thanksgiving without them, the wound was so raw. It had after all, just been a mere month after the initial blow. To know that you don't have a father for Christmas, that any and every sense of family has been changed—violently—has the potential to rattle anyone's faith.

There was a quiet sadness in my home that particular Christmas day. Despite the fact that we all knew what was going on that day—that grandpa and grandma were not coming over for dinner, that we were not invited to their place—it was the obvious smudge on the face or distracting hair out of place that we all refused to mention.

I fought the desire to openly weep that day. I had never in my life cooked a turkey, and I couldn't pick up the phone and call my mother for instructional help with it. I put a smile on my face for my daughters, tried to really make the dinner special, yet all the while my husband knew the pain I was carrying. I felt so alone and the pain in my heart was so physically real I thought I was going to die.

Having been written off by my parents, I felt stripped with no physical or spiritual inheritance. After years and years of serving my dad faithfully in the ministry, I felt lost, bewildered… I no longer had a pastor; I no longer had a father. I certainly didn't understand what God was allowing in my life.

But it was during this process that I discovered my identity. It was during this process that all fear in me was ripped out of my life. It was in this process that I was baptized with the love of the Father. How did this happen? You may ask, desperate to obtain the same results because you currently are in a painful process in your life.

In the midst of my pain *I worshiped God.* When I was at a loss for words because my reality was so bleak and dark, I worshiped God. In my loneliness—when I spent holidays by myself—an outcast in my own family, I worshiped God. I was desperate for Him. He was all that I had. It was worship and intimacy with God that took me to places in His presence that I had never imagined. I ran to my Father. I cried on His shoulder. It was in those moments of face to face conversations with my Father that He healed me and set me free from things, insecurities, fears, that had held me bound since my childhood.

I did what David did. And I am not too sure if I love or dread the dark times in my life, because there was so much pain, and truth be told, I'm yet to meet a person that eagerly awaits a process. Yet, at the same time, those were times when God held me close; it was just as the Word says, "He is close to the brokenhearted." (Psalm 34:18) Those moments with Him, I will never forget—they marked my life personally and in the ministry.

Perhaps as you read this chapter the pain you have been holding on the inside is beginning to surface. The things you thought had been settled within you are coming to mind. Maybe there is a struggle within you to let things go, if you cannot let go of situations, betrayals, disappointments, whatever the circumstance may be. Beloved reader, as long as you hold on to it, you will stay in the process unable to go onto the next great season of your life. This loving Father, He has the greatest possible plans for our lives, but He will not release anything to us until we are ready. He always has a plan, and things always get better!

Pray this prayer with me:

Heavenly Father,

I come before you today asking you to help me. Give me your grace, the ability to do what I cannot do on my own, to let go of the past. I choose to forgive those that have hurt me. I surrender the hurt, the pain, the rejection and the situation to you now and I allow you to do in me as you please. I know you turn everything around for the good, and that during this process, you are preparing me for something greater.

In Jesus' name. Amen.

PERSEVERANCE…

…never, never, never, never, never quit…

SHE SAT IN the dark living room on her sofa. Silent tears ran down her face. 'That's it. I can't do this anymore.' She thought. Her thoughts ran wild. She had just been let go of a job that was barely making allowance for the very basics in her life and that of her little son. If she only had a husband that could help her out. If she had only made better choices in life…

"You're such a loser" the voice hissed. "Just do it. Get it over with. All you have done is brought your boy shame…" She put her hands over her ears trying to drown the accusations out. She glanced over at the small prescription bottle on the end table. If she could just rest. If she could just be done with all of this. How had her life become such a disaster? She hid her face in her hands, her whole body trembling with every sob.

"I have good plans for you…" the soft, strong voice spoke clear into her very being. She looked up and around the room. Small rays of early daylight streamed through the window blinds. The voice was so audible, so clear…so gentle. She felt a sudden peace come over her. 'I'm gonna be okay. I'm gonna be okay.' She said wiping the tears from her face. 'I do believe You have good plans for me.' She whispered, remembering *the many preachings she had heard throughout the years. 'You are not done with me yet.'*

Perseverance. It is a characteristic that no child of God should go without. In the previous chapter I shared on how to overcome a process. To endure the process, any process, we must have **perseverance**. Perseverance means persistence, determination, tenacity, steadfastness, a continual effort to do or achieve despite difficulties, failures or opposition.

> "There's more to come: We continue to shout our praise even when we're hemmed in with troubles, because we know how troubles can develop passionate patience in us, and how that patience in turn forges the tempered steel of virtue, keeping us alert for whatever God will do next. In alert expectancy such as this, we're never left feeling shortchanged. Quite the contrary—we can't round up enough containers to hold everything God generously pours into our lives through the Holy Spirit!" Romans 5:3-5 (Message Translation)

To persevere we must be grounded and established in Jesus Christ, otherwise we will abandon our process and never produce fruit.

Countless times in my early years of youth ministry, the enemy tried to spew his accusations to try to make me quit. He would mockingly highlight and underline the fact that at the time I had only three teens in my youth group—all of which were rebellious. Nevertheless, I didn't quit—I couldn't quit. I had this supernatural fuel inside me that kept me going. The fuel was God's voice and His prophetic word.

I am convinced that among the many names the Holy Spirit has, one of them has to be "trainer" or "coach." I am certain those names were left out! Much like an athlete training for a competition, under the direction of the trainer, he is not allowed to quit. But the coach's voice is a constant, steady reminder that he must go on, that quitting is not an option because the prize is way too big.

I can best describe the presence of God's voice and word in my life in the most difficult—even seemingly times of defeat in my life that way—like a coach. A trainer. He has been my Trainer that has under no circumstance allowed me to give up because the prize is so incredibly big it would be foolish for me to give up!

God's voice, has been that second wind in my life. In times when I have felt the race got a little too uphill, too long, without an end in sight and I have become a bit short of breath, it has been His voice, His reminding me of promises and prophetic words that have been spoken over my life that have not allowed me to quit.

Sure, at the time, I had 3 rebellious teens—but God had shown me a generation that was on fire for Him, that would burn passionately for Him and not for the things of this world. How could I possibly quit on a loving Father that had promised me I would see such a generation? I couldn't, I wouldn't –I won't!

We must understand how powerful the voice and prophetic word of God are—it was by the direction of God's voice and word that everything we see was created. One timely word from God, beloved reader, can change the entire course of your destiny!

Inevitably there will be moments in our lives where the burden gets too heavy, but the Word of God tells us that His grace is sufficient for us, and that His power is made perfect in our weakness (2 Corinthians 12:9).

Many people don't like to think back on trials and difficult times. I often think back on those times, because it has been when I have had the most incredible encounters with Him. When I have felt Him so close, so tangibly close...He has carried me through a lot. In times when I felt my knees would buckle under the weight of the burden, He was there, and He carried me through. There were times when I just needed to be reminded, and He was faithful to remind me of every promise through prophetic word people would release, confirming things in my life; that would bring such an assurance and peace to my life. He reminded me in my prayer closet as I shut everything out in my life and hungrily sought to be alone with Him.

There is something I must say regarding prophetic word. Many believers wait for the next prophet to visit our church, or we wait for the next conference but most of the prophetic word I have received has been in my prayer closet. We need to learn as the body of Christ that we can prophesy our way through trials! We must get to the point in our walk with God that His voice is so clear in us that we are just saying what we hear Him say. In the middle of trials, what does God say? In the middle of physical pain, what is God saying? In lack, what is God saying? He certainly isn't speaking doom and gloom over our situation! We must prophesy to ourselves! The voice of God comes to us in various ways, it can simply be an inner voice, not audible, but a voice within you. It could be a voice that suddenly hits your spirit, a knowing or a dream that was dreamt.

**I push, push, push. I declare, fight, prophesy, believe.
I see it, dream it and bam! It's done!**

It has been God's voice that has fueled the perseverance in every single trial I have faced. I cannot stress enough how important this is in every believer's life. God's voice is also found in the scriptures. Many people say, "Well I've never heard God's voice, so I don't know what He is saying." One simply needs to open up the Word of God and read what God is saying! There have been many times that God's voice has come to me through a scripture I read, it was a word that I needed at that specific moment—a prophetic word.

I feel to tell a pastor that is ready to quit, because of problems in your church and home, not to give up. Dear servant of God, you cannot quit! Keep fighting the good fight of faith, because God has something amazing for you at the other side of the finish line! Persevere! As you read this, the pain in your chest is leaving and you are going to be able to breathe again! In Jesus' name!

God has placed His very own nature in us. We were made in His image and likeness—and in God's nature there is not a single thread of quitting that exists. Jesus, our Savior is the best example of perseverance. He did not give up, nor did He shy away from death unto the cross. He knew what His sacrifice would accomplish for all of humanity.

God is a Father that does not give up half way—no matter how bleak or hopeless the situation may seem, He does not quit on us. He is faithful to persevere and finish the good work He began in us! "… being confident of this, that he who began a good work in you will carry it on to completion until the day of Christ Jesus." Philippians 1:6 (NIV)

What fuels us to persevere?

- His Grace-the power of God to do what we cannot do in our own strength

- Prophetic word that has been given to us

- God's Word

- Intimacy with God

- Meditation on His Word and His promises

- Our relationship with the Father

- When we remain focused

- When we allow God to be God

- When we continually transform

- Faith

What causes us to want to quit?

- Doubt

- Unbelief

- Loss of communication with God

- No relationship with God

- Negative thoughts

- Believing lies

- Wrong friendships or associations

- Disobedience

- No faith

- Immaturity

- Lack of knowledge of the Word

- Discouragement

- Doing things in our own strength instead of leaning
  on God

What we focus on is very critical especially in times of a process. When we focus on a problem, we can convince ourselves out of the process. We convince ourselves that God won't do it, that it's too hard, that He won't answer, that things will never change.

The Word speaks to us continually about perseverance:

- "And as for you, brothers and sisters, never tire of doing what is good." 2 Thessalonians 3:13 (NIV)

- "Let us not become weary in doing good, for at the proper time we will reap a harvest if we do not give up." Galatians 6:9 (NIV)

- "For this very reason, make every effort to add to your faith goodness; and to goodness, knowledge; and to

knowledge, self-control; and to self-control, perseverance; and to perseverance, godliness;" 2 Peter 1:5-6
(NIV)

- "Be joyful in hope, patient in affliction, faithful in
  prayer." Romans 12:12 (NIV)

There are times in a process you may feel you are in the middle
of the most intense race. You may feel you are running uphill, you're
out of breath, you want to give up because there seems to be no end
in sight. At these times, it is so crucial to depend on God. Why?
Because when we depend on God we are depending on the most
loving Father. A Father that does not let us quit. He always sends
that breath, that second wind, that push to keep us going. He may
send us a dream after we have cried ourselves to sleep. He may move
someone, a pastor, a leader, a friend to give us just the right words
through a phone call or text message. He may speak to our heart in
prayer, assuring us that everything is going to be fine, because He is
God and He is in control. We may be looking up at the clouds, sighing, in the middle of a stressful day when in the middle of our exhale
His beautiful creation, the clouds, the sky remind us of just how big
He is. He is a Father, He is the Encourager, He is that Breath of Life
that will always take us past our most difficult process and into the
next season.

Pray this prayer with me:

Father,

I thank You, I love you. You are God and in control of every
season, every process in my life. Because You are with me,
I will persevere. I ask you to forgive me for ever wanting to

quit. Forgive me for doubting, for believing the lie that You won't come through and finish the good work You began in me. I trust You, and I will lean on You, on Your grace to help me to persevere!

In Jesus' name. Amen.

RESTORATION

He makes all things new...

And he who was seated on the throne said,
"Behold, I am making all things new." Revelation 21:5 (NKJV)

BIRDS SANG OUTSIDE the window waking the young woman up. Opening her eyes, she looked around the ornate room, not remembering where she was. She ran the fluffy throw between her fingers as memories of the extravagant ceremony held in her honor began to flood her mind. She ran to the large mirror across the room—and took in the image before her. Her long hair hung to her waist, she took a wavy lock to her nose and inhaled deeply. It smelled so good. How long had it been since she had washed her hair? She held out her arms and took a long sideways glance of herself—not one hole in the nightgown she was given. She smiled at her own image in awe and wonder. She reached for her stomach—the gnawing pain she usually awoke with wasn't there—of course, she had been fed the most exquisite dishes last night! It had all happened so fast. The way the countrymen found her, unrolled a scroll and read the decrees upon it. They swiftly placed her in the carriage and brought her to the palace. They read the decree so quickly she was not able to process it all. "Restore" one man read as he paused to take a look at her. "Restitution," the other announced excitedly, "reinstate" the last man smiled kindly.

"Young woman," the one holding the scroll spoke. "You have missed out on so much. You have been robbed of so much." She had stared at him blankly. "You have no idea who you are, do you?" He took her hand pulling her up off of the familiar corner she sat in begging for food or money. "Come, your Father is anxiously awaiting your return."

I don't know that there is anything that touches the heart of the Father more than when He sees His children restored. "Ah, yes, that's just the way I always had in my heart for them to live." He must say.

Merriam Webster's dictionary defines restoration as reinstatement and restitution. Simply defined "restoration" means to bring us back to our original state; with nothing missing and nothing broken. Because the original state, the state you and I were created in, was just that—we were made whole—with nothing missing and we were also made complete—with nothing broken. Before we experienced life, pain, trials, divorce, division and sickness...the state God created us in was one of nothing missing from us...no piece of our hearts missing and no part of our innermost being broken.

In God's original plan, in heaven, it is for us to be healed, joyful, united, complete, whole, lacking nothing, prosperous, strong, fruitful, living in abundance, free, living lives full of purpose, fulfilling our calling on this earth and to bring everything that is available in heaven here to earth.

It is the plan of our Heavenly Father to fulfill the call of God over our lives. God is committed to make certain we finish the race. He is a faithful Father. He doesn't throw a football pass and watch on the sidelines hoping that we catch and score in life. No! He is faithful every step of the way! Perhaps you have experienced much loss, loss of family, loss of health, loss of finances, the loss of a ministry or even a child to the world. God is faithful. He is the Restorer of all things! He knows exactly what He is doing with our lives. We must trust that whatever has been broken or lost in our lives, He will take care of.

The God that created you knows exactly at what moment to come in and restore all which has been lost and broken in your life! He knows us—intimately—He knows exactly what we need and when we need it. He knows.

Jeremiah 29:11 (NKJV) says, "For I know the plans I have for you," declares the Lord, "plans to prosper you and not to harm you, plans to give you hope and a future." We all love this scripture, we know it by heart. These were actually the words God sent His prophet Jeremiah to tell all the people that were at the time in exile. The Israelites were in a land that was not their own, they had been carried off as captives from Jerusalem to Babylon. At the time that these words were spoken over them by the prophet, they still had another 70 years to go in exile! Imagine that! Have you ever felt like that? You are in a place, a season of your life that you want OUT like yesterday. You see no way out, you see no improvement. God is telling you, "I know the plans I have for you. Be still, don't worry, don't fret. I know it looks bad right now, I know you don't want to be here in this place but the plans I have for you are so good. They are plans to bring you hope and prosperity."

God's original plan, His will for us is to receive all He has provided for us; all Jesus won at the Cross. Healing, deliverance, prosperity and restoration are included in what Jesus won for us on the Cross. For this reason, we don't have to settle. We don't have to think that God won't finish what He began.

The Word of God has the most spectacular stories. What is even more astounding is that they are not only spectacular but they are historically accurate. The story of Joseph is perhaps one of those stories that will get any one fist-pumping at the end. His story is found in the book of Genesis chapters 37-50. Joseph was the youngest of 10 brothers, and his father loved him deeply and favored him over his brothers. Needless to say, this young man faced a lot of jealousy and hatred from his brothers. To heighten the tension between him and his brothers, this young man shared a couple of dreams he should have probably kept to himself. God was speaking to Joseph about the great destiny He had for him, but not everyone rejoiced with him. Joseph's brothers hated him so much that they plotted his murder, later changing their plans and selling him off as a slave to foreigners. After Joseph was hauled off to a distant land as a slave, he was accused of rape when he refused to succumb to the sexual advances his boss's wife offered. He was thrown into prison for this alleged rape, but even in prison the man excelled in everything he did. It almost seemed as if he was on his way out of prison after accurately interpreting some dreams in prison, yet the favor was quickly forgotten and so was he. Many of us would have shouted at the top of our lungs, "But God! I don't understand! You told me I had a great destiny!" Yet throughout the 13 years of trial, Joseph humbly served God.

We must understand that God is the ultimate game-changer. He can at any moment change the circumstances in our lives. As a matter of fact, while you read this, heaven is busy at work preparing the most incredible breakthrough in your life. God brought about a sudden change in Joseph's life after 13 years of suffering. You may be right in the middle of your trial, but God is very much aware of you, as He was of Joseph. He has not forgotten you. With the most amazing turn of events in a moment in Joseph's life, he was remembered by one of the men he did the favor of interpreting a dream for. This man's boss needed a dream interpreted. This man's boss happened to be Pharaoh—the ruler of all of Egypt. At the end of the story, Joseph is so respected that he is the second in command of all of Egypt. That is not all beloved, some of us have perhaps reached a place of blessing in our lives and that is good. Yet, God always has more. Remember Joseph's jealous brothers? Well, they faced a famine in their land and they traveled to none other than the land of Egypt for help.

Joseph's response to them was truly a merciful one, full of wisdom and forgiveness. The following words best describe his entire story:

"You intended to harm me, but God intended it for good to accomplish what is now being done, the saving of many lives..." Genesis 50:20 (NKJV)

God had a plan for Joseph's life all along. Beloved, God's plans are always greater than an individual's life. He not only had in mind to restore Joseph and his brothers, but God had in mind to save the people of Israel from a famine that would have surely wiped them out. The plan of God was revealed since the beginning. The plan of the enemy was to destroy Joseph's destiny, his calling, his purpose, his dream... but God turned everything around for the good.

God uses all things for our good, Romans 8:28 says, "And we know that in all things God works for the good of those who love him, who have been called according to his purpose."

In the middle of the process we undergo, as we endure trials and situations just as Joseph did, God forms our character.

God's detailed plan for our lives is to bring us to the place of complete restoration. Perhaps you, dear reader, have gone through so much that you cannot fathom what the restored you would look like, but let me tell you, the restored you looks glorious.

The restored you begins in the place of forgiveness...

Joseph forgave his brothers for all the harm, the pain and suffering he endured because of their jealousy. What they did to him was terribly cruel. Perhaps you have endured suffering and pain, God is not so much interested in if it was fair, or not fair, He is more actively involved in leading you to forgive. When you forgive, He begins the new in you.

In my journey, as painful as the rejection was, as lonely as the first holidays were without my family, as disconcerting as it was to not know where to take a congregation because I had been abruptly ousted from my parent's church...I had to forgive. I had to allow God to mold me and form and develop my character in order to receive the inheritance.

It has been almost five years since the day I received the visit to my front door warning me never to go back to my father's church or else I would face the risk of being arrested. It has been quite a journey. But there is one place that I continually visited throughout that particular trial—and any trial in my life really. It is the place where my Father and I meet. The place where I pour tears as I worship and He holds me close. I imagine Joseph had such encounters with the God of his fathers. I have wholeheartedly forgiven my earthly father, all my family, in fact for everything that happened back then. God has restored us to the father-daughter relationship that I wept for. We are able to share meals again, spend holidays together again, laugh and enjoy each other's company again. God is the restorer of all things broken, and along with restoration God brings restitution. Five years ago, we had no place to congregate, today we have a beautiful building where over 2,000 souls gather weekly to worship God. We recently became owners of over 10 acres of beautiful land where God's future temple will be built. And my father, the man that once said he disowned me as a daughter and left me without a place to congregate, recently informed me that the building and land where he has his church is my inheritance. God's ways are beautiful and much greater and higher than our own.

So often people run from the process—they run before allowing God to finish the work, they quit too soon. Our restoration may be right around the corner, but we give up too soon. Many run from the process refusing to forgive, allowing bitterness and resentment to take over their lives. They live in self-pity; they live in defeat and unforgiveness. They are bitter, angry, frustrated, carrying around the "poor old me" syndrome. These people repeat cycle after cycle and they fail to surrender. They don't surrender the pain, the hurt, the unforgiveness—all the contrary, they hold on to it. They refuse to humble themselves and forgive the offender. They hold on to the past, they hold on to the hurt, the betrayal, the abandonment and rejection.

Sadly, individuals such as these never reach their purpose; they never reach their calling, the only thing they reach is the repeat button in their lives setting off another destructive, stagnant cycle.

Beloved, if only you could see what God has for you on the other side of forgiveness. If only you could behold the image of yourself fully restored with nothing missing and nothing broken. God has the most beautiful destiny ready for you.

Dear reader, I have the certainty that as you say this final prayer with me that things in your life will begin to shift. As you wholeheartedly pronounce the words of this prayer, God at the very same instant is turning all things in your life around for the good.

Say this prayer with all your heart:

Father,

I ask You to forgive me for holding on to the pain and offense. I ask that You would give me the grace to forgive _____ (say the name of the person or people you need to forgive) for _____ (tell God what was done to hurt you). I forgive them with all my heart, I release them and the painful memories that I have held onto for too long. I let go of my past. I let go of the pain. I let go of the offense. I forgive them, Father. I want to be free and ready to receive all that You have for me. Thank You, Father, because You are restoring and making all things new in my life.

In Jesus' name. Amen.